W9-APC-944

HOME RUN HERO!

Mark McGwire

BY JOE LAYDEN

SCHOLASTIC INC.

New York Toronto London Auckland Sydney
Mexico City New Delhi Hong Kong

About the Author

Joe Layden has written nearly two dozen books for children and adults, including titles such as *NBA Game Day, Against the Odds, The Kobe Bryant Story,* and *Dribble, Shoot, Score!* He is also the author of *Women in Sports: The Complete Book on the World's Greatest Female Athletes, The Art of Magic,* and *America on Wheels.* Mr. Layden frequently visits school classrooms to discuss the craft of writing with students. He lives in upstate New York with his wife, Susan, and their daughter, Emily.

Photography credits: Mark McGwire cover: Jed Jacobsohn/Allsport. Sammy Sosa cover: Elsa Hasch/Allsport. Page 1: David Klutho/ Sports Illustrated/Time Inc.; page 2 Rich Pilling/MLB Photos; page 3: Eric Draper/AP/Wide World; page 4: Ed Reinke/AP Photo/Wide World; page 5: Green/Sports Illustrated/Time Inc.; page 6: Tom Di-Pace/Sports Illustrated/Time Inc.; page 7: Gary Dineen/AP/Wide World; pages 8-9: Reuters/Tim Parker/Archive; page 10: Jed Jacobsohn/Allsport; page 11: Kent Horner/AP/ Wide World; page 12: Matthew Stockman/Allsport; page 13: Reuters/Scott Olson/Archive Photos; page 14: David Durochik/MLB Photos; page 14 inset: Elsa Hasch/Allsport; page 15 Matthew Stockman/Allsport; page 16: Stephen Green/MLB Photos.

If you purchased this book without a cover, you should be aware that this book is stolen property. It was reported as "unsold and destroyed" to the publisher, and neither the author nor the publisher has received any payment for this "stripped book."

No part of this publication may be reproduced in whole or in part, or stored in a retrieval system, or transmitted in any form or by any means, electronic, mechanical, photocopying, recording, or otherwise, without written permission of the publisher. For information regarding permission, write to Scholastic Inc., Attention: Permissions Department, 555 Broadway, New York, NY 10012.

ISBN 0-439-05746-9

Copyright © 1999 by Scholastic Inc.
All rights reserved. Published by Scholastic Inc.
SCHOLASTIC and associated logos are trademarks and/or registered trademarks of Scholastic Inc.

12 11 10 9   1 2 3 4/0

Printed in the U.S.A.

First Scholastic printing, January 1999

For Sam — A Little Slugger

HOME RUN HERO!

Mark McGwire

1

A Night to Remember

September 8, 1998

As Mark McGwire strolled from the on-deck circle to the batter's box in the bottom of the fourth inning, a wave of excitement washed over Busch Stadium. It began as a low buzz and quickly grew into a deafening roar. The crowd stood and applauded. Thousands of flash-bulbs flickered and popped. For a moment, time seemed to stand still.

In his first at bat Mark had grounded out. But there was a feeling of anticipation in the air as he stepped to the plate in the fourth inning. Not a single person in Busch Stadium remained seated. The children of Roger Maris, who had made the trip to St. Louis in anticipation of seeing their father's record broken, stood close to the railing along the first-base line. In right field, Sammy Sosa slapped a fist into his glove.

At the plate, Mark McGwire flexed his 20-inch biceps and held the bat high. Though the stick was 34½ inches of northern white ash and weighed a meaty 33 ounces, Mark waved it effortlessly, like a toothpick. At precisely 8:18 P.M., Central Time, Chicago pitcher Steve Traschel went into his windup. As the ball whistled toward the plate, Mark's body uncoiled. There was the sweet sound of wood meeting leather. A crack of the bat. And then a roar.

It was the sound of history being made.

In this setting it was hard to imagine that the sport of baseball had ever been ill. Just four years earlier a labor dispute had nearly ruined the game. A season was canceled, and fans were disappointed, angry, and disillusioned. The wounds caused by the strike of 1994 were slow to heal. Some people wondered if baseball would regain its status as America's national pastime.

But on this late summer night in St. Louis, Missouri, baseball had never seemed healthier. Attendance was climbing. Records were being shattered. Old fans were returning to ballparks, and new fans were tagging along. The 1998 season had already been one of the most memorable in the history of baseball — but the best was still to come. You see, the Great Home Run Race was not yet over.

"The whole country seems to be involved in this," McGwire, the St. Louis Cardinals star first baseman, had said. "It's exciting. It puts baseball back on the map as a sport."

Of all the records in baseball, none was considered more untouchable than the single-season mark for home runs. But all records are made to be broken. In 1927 the legendary New York Yankees slugger Babe Ruth hit 60 home runs in a single season. That record stood for thirty-four years until another Yankee, Roger Maris, hit 61 in 1961. Now, thirty-seven years later, Mark McGwire was dramatically giving chase.

Big Mac wasn't alone, either. Both he and Chicago Cubs outfielder Sammy Sosa had been hammering the ball all season. As they swung their way into the record books, they developed a friendship as well as a rivalry. They cheered for each other on and off the field. They applauded each other's towering home runs. Together they captured the imagination of baseball fans across the country. It seemed certain that at least one of these men would break Maris' record. The only question was . . . who would be first?

By September 8, Mark had the edge. He had belted his 61st home run to tie Maris' record one day earlier, in a game against the Cubs. Then, he hit historic number 62. Sammy, meanwhile, was stuck at 58. But Sammy was far from finished. The showdown was about to begin.

2

Growing Up

At 6 feet 5, 250 pounds, Mark McGwire is physically one of the biggest players in Major League Baseball. Although he's worked hard to become strong and fit, his size is at least partially a natural gift from his father John McGwire. It also seems likely that Mark inherited his dad's strength of character and his will to succeed.

Today, John McGwire is a robust 6 feet 3 inches, 225 pounds. His childhood, however, was a different story. When he was just seven years old, John contracted polio, a disease that attacks the central nervous system and sometimes leaves its victims crippled. He spent six painful months in a hospital bed, and was left with one leg several inches shorter than the other. He was forced to wear a brace on his right leg.

Despite his illness, John became a devoted athlete. He was a boxer in college and later, an accomplished golfer. Even now, at the age of sixty-one, he rides his bicycle for several hours each week. In addition to his athletic achievements, John McGwire was a standout in the classroom. He earned exceptional grades and eventually became a successful dentist.

A Big Family

John and his wife, Ginger, settled in southern California and began raising a family. They had five children — all boys. Mark, the middle child, was born October 1, 1963. Like his brothers, he was a big kid with an enormous appetite. Ginger spent a lot of her time in the kitchen. She often *tripled* recipes just to make sure she didn't run out of food at dinnertime!

Mark is the most famous of the McGwire children, but he is not the only successful athlete. Younger brother Dan McGwire went to college on a football scholarship and later played quarterback for the Miami Dolphins and the Seattle Seahawks in the National Football League. Older brother Bob McGwire played on his college golf team and older brother Mike McGwire played varsity golf and soccer in high school. The youngest of the boys, Jay, was a great all-around athlete whose competitive career was cut short by an eye injury. Today, though, Jay is still devoted to sports and fitness. He works as a personal trainer. Each McGwire boy grew up to be a big man. In fact, they're all at least 6 feet 3 inches tall and weigh at least 220 pounds.

Although Mark is a record-breaking slugger who appears to be headed to the Baseball Hall of Fame, his early years as an athlete were sometimes frustrating. When he was seven years old, his father *refused* to let him play Little League baseball! John McGwire liked sports and wanted his kids to enjoy athletic competition, but he didn't want them to begin playing seriously at too young an age. He had heard stories about incompetent coaches and meddling parents. He was worried that his son would develop bad habits. Mark would have to wait.

"When I told him he couldn't play, he cried and cried and cried," John once said in an interview with *The Sporting News*. But the following year John gave in and allowed little Mark to play. In his very first trip to the plate, eight-year-old Mark hit a home run off a twelve-year-old pitcher. Even then, he was strong for his age.

But what really impressed John was his son's knowledge of the game.

"He had a sense of how to play," John said. "He knew where to position players. He just knew. It was spine-tingling, his understanding of the game at such an early age."

Mark also played golf, basketball, and soccer when he was growing up. He liked most sports and seemed to be pretty good at everything he tried. Although he was a big kid, he was not really at a physical advantage on the playing field. In fact, he had some obstacles to overcome. For one thing, Mark had very poor vision (he says he's practically "blind" without his contact lenses or glasses!). For another, he was prone to illness. When he was a sophomore at Damien High School, outside Los Angeles, he came down with a severe case of mononucleosis. Mark was so tired and sick that he actually quit baseball and began concentrating on golf, a sport that isn't as physically demanding.

Golf is also not a team sport, and that appealed to Mark. He was an intensely shy kid, and he liked the idea of being out on a golf course by himself, working on his game. "I was always the kind of kid who liked to sit in the back of the room and just blend in," Mark told *Sports Illustrated*. "I was always just a basic athlete, nothing extraordinary. But I was a hard worker. And I liked to do a lot of that work where people couldn't see me. The thing I liked about golf was that you were the only one there to blame when something went wrong."

But after a while Mark began to miss baseball. It had always been his favorite sport. Ginger McGwire remembers her son watching games on television when he was just a toddler. By the time he was in grade school he was telling anyone who would listen that he wanted to be a big-league ballplayer when he grew up. Now, with only two years left in high school, it was time for him to either give up on that dream, or pursue it with all his heart.

Mark dusted off his glove and returned to the baseball field.

All-America

Like Babe Ruth, who was a star pitcher for the Boston Red Sox before he became a star slugger for the New York Yankees, Mark first made his baseball mark on the mound. By the time he graduated from Damien High in 1981, he was one of the top pitching prospects in southern California. The Montreal Expos liked Mark so much they selected him in the eighth round of the major league draft. The Expos weren't the only ones who wanted Mark. He was also offered a full athletic scholarship by the University of Southern California (USC). It was tempting to go pro right away but Mark decided to go on to college.

As a freshman at USC, Mark won as many games as he lost (his record was 4–4) and compiled a respectable ERA (earned run average) of 3.04. He had decent control of his pitches and a fastball that hovered near the 90-mph mark. He was the best right-hander on the team. He even allowed fewer runs than his teammate, Randy Johnson, who would go on to become one of the best pitchers in Major League Baseball!

Still, it was obvious to at least one of Mark's coaches that he was wasting his time and talent on the mound. When Mark played for the Anchorage Glacier Pilots in the Alaska summer league in 1982, he was asked to play first base. The team's coach, Ron Vaughn, was also an assistant at USC. Vaughn had been impressed by Mark's power and timing during batting practice sessions. He knew Mark could be a good pitcher. But he believed Mark had the potential to be a *great* hitter. Vaughn helped Mark adjust his stance and his grip. Everything else came naturally.

By the time he returned to USC, Mark was one of the best power hitters in college baseball. He batted .319 as a sophomore and .387 as a junior. The USC record for home runs in a career was 32. Mark hit that many in his junior year *alone*! In the spring of 1984 he was named first-team All-America and College Player of the Year. A few months later he helped the United States win a gold medal in baseball at the Summer Olympics in Los Angeles.

You wouldn't get much of this information from Mark, since he has always been reluctant to talk about his own accomplishments. He is a genuinely modest man who doesn't like to display any of his awards in his home. Even as a boy he used to hide his trophies in a dresser drawer because he was embarrassed by the attention they might attract. In the USC media guide Mark even declined to fill out the section for "athletic accomplishments." Instead, he left it blank.

But as he prepared to leave USC and begin a professional career, it was obvious that Mark McGwire would no longer be able to hide.

3

Big League Ballplayer

The Oakland Athletics selected Mark in the first round of the 1984 free-agent draft. Although he had one year of college eligibility remaining, he decided that the time was right to turn professional. As the tenth player selected in the draft, he was offered a good contract. The money came in handy, since Mark was about to marry his girlfriend, Kathy Hughes. The two had met a few years earlier, when Mark was playing at USC and Kathy was the team's batgirl.

Most kids have some trouble adjusting to the professional world after leaving college, and Mark was no different. In the spring of 1985 the A's assigned him to their Class-A minor league team in Modesto, California. Class A is the lowest level of professional baseball, but it's still populated by talented players. Mark quickly discovered that he'd have to work a lot harder than he had in college. In the first few weeks of the season he couldn't even hit a single, let alone a home run. He was striking out a lot and making errors in the field. It was the first time in Mark's baseball career that he had ever really struggled, and he soon became dispirited. He even thought about giving up baseball.

As Kathy recalled during an interview with *Sports Illustrated*, "I can remember lying in bed in the middle of the night, and Mark saying 'I can't hit the baseball anymore. I'm done. I've lost it. I've got to quit.'"

But he didn't quit. Even though he wasn't hitting the ball consistently, Mark displayed flashes of brilliance. Just as he does today, he thrilled fans with his monstrous home runs during batting practice. And he worked extremely hard to improve his fielding. He stayed late after practice. He showed up early on game days. He took hundreds of ground balls each week in an effort to become the best defensive player he could.

The hard work eventually paid off. Mark began hitting more home runs and striking out less often. Over the course of two years he progressed steadily through the A's minor league system. He graduated from Class A to Class AA and finally wound up with the team's Class-AAA club in Tacoma, Washington. In two full seasons Mark hit .298 and averaged 25 home runs and 109 runs batted in. He did, however, continue to struggle in the field. He committed 41 errors in 1986. But that was primarily because he was trying to learn a new position, third base. (Infielders often rotate positions, to see which they're strongest at.)

The A's promoted Mark to the majors at the end of the 1986 season. He didn't make much of an impact. In fact, he sometimes looked like a player who was in over his head. He struck out eighteen times in eighteen games. His batting average was an embarrassing .189. But A's manager Tony La Russa saw something in Mark. He liked the kid's power and talent. He also liked his attitude. With a little time and effort, La Russa thought, this player could be something special.

Rookie of the Year

During spring training in 1987, Mark played well enough to earn a spot on the A's roster as a reserve, or back-up infielder. But shortly after the season began, he was named the team's starting first baseman.

Unfortunately, Mark did not play well in the first few weeks of the season. His batting average was only .167. For a while, it appeared as though Mark might be sent back to the minor leagues. He was discouraged.

But Mark was lucky. The A's manager continued to believe in him. La Russa felt that Mark's fielding had improved a lot. He also liked the way Mark attacked the ball at the plate. Eventually, La Russa felt, Mark would get into a rhythm. When that happened, there would be no doubt about whether Mark had the ability to make it as a pro.

"One great thing about being an everyday ballplayer is you don't make a season in a week, or a season in a month," McGwire said in an interview with *Sports Illustrated* during his rookie season. "You make a season in a season."

That first season, 1987, turned out to be one of the most memorable in the history of baseball. Mark's confidence improved after those first few shaky weeks and he soon began ripping the ball out of the park like no rookie before him. By the Fourth of July he had belted a league-leading 30 home runs. He was the first rookie in the history of the game to hit 30 home runs before the All-Star break. He was also the first rookie to hit 5 home runs in a doubleheader.

Baseball fans were captivated by Mark's awesome power. It wasn't long before people started talking about the possibility of him breaking one of the most respected records in baseball: Roger Maris' single-season mark for home runs. It wasn't unreasonable. After all, Mark had needed just seventy-three games to hit his first 30 home runs. Why couldn't he hit 32 more in the last eighty-nine games?

As Mark himself pointed out, however, baseball is a long season. It stretches out over nearly six months. For every streak there is usually a slump. The trick is to stay calm and consistent. So, when reporters pressed Mark about the home run record, he usually just shrugged and said, "No sense thinking about that yet."

The media pressure continued after the All-Star break. Mark hit his 39th home run on August 14 to break the fifty-seven-year-old record for most home runs in a season by a rookie. And with each game the crowd of media representatives around his locker grew larger. During batting practice and after games, hundreds of fans surrounded him and asked for his autograph.

Baseball fans are fascinated by home run hitters — especially big, powerful home run hitters. Mark was leaner then than he is now, but he still was an impressive man. He was 6 feet 5 inches, 225 pounds. Back in those days, he always seemed to have a scowl on his face. Mark wasn't unhappy. He was just very serious about his job. And, the shy kid had grown into a shy man. He was uncomfortable being the center of attention.

"I never wanted to be in the public eye," he later said to a reporter, explaining that all he ever wanted, when he was away from the ballpark, was to be with his family and friends. But Mark couldn't even go into a restaurant without being bothered. Everybody knew him as Mark McGwire, the baseball player. He didn't want to be just the baseball player. He wanted to be himself.

Mark even found it difficult to express himself when he hit a home run. A lot of players pump their fists and stroll casually around the bases, soaking in the applause. Mark was never like that. He trotted around the bases with his head down. He showed almost no emotion, in part, he once explained, because he has a lot of respect for pitchers and didn't want to embarrass them by celebrating.

Among Mark's teammates on the A's was Reggie Jackson, one of the game's best power hitters. Jackson was also a great clutch player. His nickname was "Mr. October," because he always excelled in the play-offs and World Series. Jackson was a stylish player who loved attention. When he hit a home run, he would often stand at the plate and watch the ball soar. His home run trot was elegant. It was a performance. When Mark would return to the dugout after hitting a homer, he was often greeted by Jackson. The veteran would kid the rookie about his trot. He offered to help Mark add a little style to his routine. But Mark wasn't interested. He just wanted to play the game.

Mark slowed down in the final two months, but he still had a great rookie season. He wound up with a league-leading 49 home runs and 118 RBIs (runs batted in). His batting average was a respectable .289. When the season was over, he became the first player in fifteen years to be chosen unanimously as American League Rookie of the Year.

Mark McGwire, the private citizen, also earned the respect of fans. He could have become the first rookie to hit 50 home runs in a season. But he missed the last game of the season so that he could be at Kathy's side when she gave birth to their first child. They named him Matt, and he has since become Mark's best friend in the world. To Mark, skipping that final game wasn't a difficult decision at all.

"I'll have other chances to hit fifty home runs," he explained. "But I'll never have another chance to see my son being born."

4

Hard Times

By the spring of 1988, Mark was one of the most popular and admired players in baseball. But he was feeling pressure. By playing so well as a rookie, he had set a standard that could be hard to match in the future. He was also part of a team that was expected to be one of the best in baseball. The A's back then were led by Mark and José Canseco, another big, young player who could hit the ball a long way.

Mark and José became known as the "Bash Brothers," not only because they bashed a lot of home runs, but because they liked to bash their forearms together after one of them had homered. It became a routine that was copied throughout the league, and by children all over the country. If Mark hit a home run, José would be waiting for him at the plate. José would hold his arms up, and Mark would give him a forearm high five.

That was the closest thing to a celebration that Mark would allow himself.

From 1988 through 1990, the A's were one of the best teams in baseball. They won three consecutive American League pennants. In 1989 they won the World Series.

Ironically, despite the team's success, this was one of the most difficult periods in Mark's life. He found it really hard to adjust to being a celebrity. He was young and suddenly rich and famous. Everybody wanted a piece of him. Because he was a professional baseball player, Mark spent a lot of time on the road. Eventually his marriage began to crack under the strain. He and Kathy divorced in the fall of 1988, shortly before that year's World Series. Looking back on it now, Mark believes he was just too young and immature to accept the responsibility of marriage.

"Sometimes I wish I could go back and do my marriage all over again," he told a writer from *Sports Illustrated* in the summer of 1998. "It would be a lot better. I think if I'd known [then] what I know now, it would have lasted."

Falling Into a Slump

Mark was starting to have problems at the ballpark, as well as at home. In 1988 he had 32 home runs and 99 RBIs. His batting average slipped to .260. Thanks largely to José Canseco (who led the league in home runs and RBIs) and a strong pitching staff, the A's were able to win the American League pennant. In the World Series, however, they were badly beaten by the Los Angeles Dodgers, four games to one.

The 1988 Series was a disaster for Mark. He had just one hit in eighteen at bats. But that was only the beginning of a downward spiral that would last nearly four years.

It wasn't as if he completely fell apart. Mark continued to hit long balls and drive in runs at a respectable rate. From 1988 through 1991 he averaged more than 31 home runs and 94 RBIs per season. But he was wildly inconsistent. His batting average fell to .231 in 1989 and finally bottomed out at .201 in 1991.

There were a lot of rumors about Mark back then. He had been hit hard by wild pitches on a few occasions, and some observers quietly wondered if he had lost his nerve in the batter's box. They thought he was afraid to face the league's best fastball pitchers. But that wasn't Mark's problem at all. He had simply lost the ability to focus. He was having so many problems in his personal life that he couldn't concentrate on baseball. He was unhappy with himself and his life, and that contributed to his below par performance on the field.

At the same time, opposing pitchers were beginning to understand him better and throw him tougher pitches. Mark was no longer seeing the same kind of pitches he saw as a rookie. He had to be more patient at the plate. He had to work harder. Unfortunately, he was reluctant to do either of those things.

"Pitchers made adjustments to me," Mark said in an interview with *Sport* magazine. "But I wasn't making adjustments to them. I didn't realize the game was mental until my terrible season in '91. It taught me to wake up and smell the coffee. Sometimes you get to a certain level and you think you don't have to work as hard. I'm not saying I didn't work. I'm saying I could have worked harder. And I had a lot of personal problems on top of that. When you get distracted from what you love to do, failure usually follows."

"Failure" is probably too strong a word. After all, Mark did win a Gold Glove for his exceptional fielding in 1990. (In a typically humble gesture, he gave the trophy to his optometrist, since Mark felt he couldn't have won the award without his contact lenses.) And he helped the A's win a memorable World Series in 1989.

That year marked the first time the A's and their Bay Area rivals, the San Francisco Giants, had ever met in the Series. But that's not the only reason it made history. After the A's won the first two games in Oakland, the Series shifted to San Francisco's Candlestick Park. During pregame warm-ups, a massive earthquake rocked the Bay Area. Candlestick Park shook and swayed. The power went out, and the game was postponed.

Before long, word of the quake's damage began to trickle in. As it turned out, fans at Candlestick had been very lucky — no one died there. But in other parts of the city, sixty-seven people lost their lives and billions of dollars of damage was caused. Fay Vincent, the commissioner of Major League Baseball, announced that the World Series would be postponed indefinitely so that the people of Oakland and San Francisco could concentrate on far more serious matters, such as rebuilding after the earthquake.

While some observers felt the World Series should have been canceled in honor of the victims who had died in the earthquake, most people were in favor of its completion. They thought it would be good for the city's morale. So, after a delay of ten days, the Series resumed.

The A's won Game 3 by a score of 13–7. The turning point in the game came in the fourth inning. The A's had a 4–3 lead, but the Giants had two runners on base and were threatening to go ahead. With two outs, Mark McGwire made a diving stop on a hard ground ball hit by San Francisco's Pat Sheridan. Mark flipped the ball to A's pitcher Dave Stewart, who was covering first, to end the inning. It was one of the best defensive plays of the entire World Series. The A's went on to win easily, and then completed a sweep in Game 4.

Winning a World Series ring and a Gold Glove were tremendous accomplishments for Mark. Still, by 1991 his career and his life were not in the best shape. As his batting average plummeted, he began tinkering with his swing. One of his coaches told him he was trying to hit too many home runs. Mark was a natural right-handed power hitter who pulled most balls to left field. But his hitting instructor wanted him to try punching the ball to the opposite field once in a while. This felt strange to Mark, but he decided to give it a try.

The experiment failed badly. Mark became even more confused. His batting average continued to drop. La Russa was unhappy with Mark's performance, but he also felt bad for him. The manager pulled Mark from the lineup in the final days of the 1991 season so that Mark's batting average couldn't slip below the .200 mark. La Russa wanted to save a player he believed in from embarrassment.

The manager also wanted to make sure that Mark's value as a player didn't slip any further. You see, the A's were thinking seriously about trading Mark. There was just one problem. No one really wanted him.

Mark was twenty-seven years old. And it looked like his career might be over.

5

The Road to Recovery

Mark was so discouraged during the summer of 1991 that he seriously considered quitting baseball altogether. He was convinced that his career was over and that no one would miss him if he left. Not even the fans in Oakland. He was actually *booed* whenever he came to the plate. He was even harrassed at home. Mark lived near an elementary school in Alamo, California, at the time. One day, while he was sitting by his pool, he heard a group of children yelling across a nearby fence. When Mark stood up, the kids shouted, "McGwire, you stink!"

Mark was devastated. It was one thing to be criticized by the media. It was quite another to be heckled by a group of children. Maybe it really *was* time to hang up his spikes.

"For the first time, I disliked baseball," Mark recalled in an interview with *Sports Illustrated.* "It was frustrating trying to climb out of a hole that got deeper and deeper. I started joking in the clubhouse that I was going to shoot pool for a living, or maybe become a policeman. I was kidding, but there was an element of truth in what I was saying."

After the season Mark jumped into his car and took a long ride down the California coast to his home in Los Angeles. Along the way he asked himself a lot of tough questions. By the time the ride was over, Mark had decided that he had to make some major changes in his life. He began seeing a psychiatrist to help sort out his feelings.

"That was the turning point in my life as a person and as a professional ballplayer," Mark told *Sport* magazine. "Seeking help made me the person I am today. It made me find out what I'm all about. I believe that anyone who confronts his problems succeeds."

One of the things Mark discovered was his true athletic purpose. For the past several years he had been trying to become a different type of baseball player. He had changed his stance and his swing in an attempt to raise his batting average. He was a natural home run hitter, but he

was trying to hit singles. From now on, Mark re-
solved, that would change. "I decided I wouldn't
fight it because that's what I am, a home run
hitter," he said. "That's what God put me here to
be."

The Comeback Kid

The Mark McGwire of 1992 looked a lot like
the pre-slump Mark McGwire of 1987. In the
first forty-three games of the season he hit 17
home runs. Once again he was on pace to break
the record for most homers in a season. At the
All-Star break, he led the American League in
home runs and RBIs.

Mark was playing better because his attitude
had changed. He was also working harder than
he ever had in his life. In the off-season he
moved in with his brother Jay, a former body-
builder. With Jay's help, Mark began lifting
weights seriously. He spent hours in the gym almost every single day. By the time the season
began, Mark had added 25 pounds of muscle to
his frame. He now weighed 250 pounds. Weight
lifting increased Mark's strength and flexibility.
It also gave him confidence.

"Weight training just makes you feel better
about yourself," Mark has said. "When I started

to see the changes in my body, it made me feel a lot more positive."

The A's felt pretty good about Mark, too. He finished the season with 42 home runs and 104 RBIs, despite missing three weeks because of injuries. His batting average was a solid .268.

Unfortunately, injuries also kept Mark out of the lineup for most of the 1993 and 1994 seasons. He had to have foot surgery twice. He was bothered by a nagging back injury. Mark played in only seventy-four games in two years. While he was in the lineup, though, he actually played quite well. His batting average over those two seasons was a healthy .283. He also hit 18 home runs. That may not sound like many, until you consider that Mark only had 219 at bats. So he was hitting a homer in every twelve trips to the plate. That was nearly the same rate he had achieved during his sensational rookie season.

To Mark's credit, he didn't let the injuries get him down. He kept working out. And he did his homework. He sat behind home plate during games and watched opposing pitchers, to learn their strengths and weaknesses. He studied other hitters that he admired. Just because he couldn't be on the field didn't mean Mark couldn't improve.

"I'm a firm believer that things happen for a reason," Mark once told a reporter from *The*

Sporting News. "I know that just watching the games those years made me a better hitter. I learned a lot just watching. I learned much more of the mental side of the game. I learned how to stay positive."

Mark missed five weeks because of injuries in 1995. But he still had a very good season. He batted .274 with 39 home runs and 90 RBIs. A few months later Mark was tested once again. He injured his left foot during spring training. Doctors told him he would have to undergo serious physical therapy and that he would miss the first few weeks of the 1996 season. Mark was disappointed. He had been injured so many times in the past few years that he was beginning to wonder whether his body was trying to send him a message.

So once again, Mark thought about early retirement. But not for long. He looked to his father for inspiration and convinced himself that the pain he was feeling really wasn't all that bad, especially when compared to what John McGwire had endured. Deep down, Mark also knew that he wasn't ready to leave baseball behind. He was only thirty-two years old. More important, he still loved the game.

So Mark worked hard to recover from his injury. He was back in the lineup by the end of April. Pretty soon he was swatting home runs at a remarkable rate. In fact, 1996 was the finest season in Mark's career. He missed thirty-two games because of injuries, but still finished the year with 52 home runs and 113 RBIs. Mark was only the 14th player in major league history to hit 50 home runs in a season. And no one had reached that mark in so few appearances at the plate. Mark averaged 1 home run in every 8.13 at bats. Not even the great Babe Ruth had hit home runs at such a clip.

When the season was over, most people wondered what Mark might have accomplished if he had been healthy through the whole season. Maybe he would have hit 60 home runs . . . or more. Maybe he would have passed Babe Ruth and Roger Maris.

Mark refused to be drawn into such conversations. He just went about his business in his usual humble manner. He was simply happy to be playing so well.

A Good Father

Mark was also pleased with the way his personal life had improved. He and his ex-wife, Kathy, were now getting along extremely well. Both were committed to providing a loving home for their son. Matthew McGwire lived with his mother and stepfather, just a few miles from Mark's house.

Matt had a chance to see his dad almost every day during the off-season. They developed a very close relationship. In fact, as most baseball fans now know, Mark and Matt are not just father and son.

They are best friends.

As Mark has said, "Everything I do in life is for Matt."

6

A Gentle Giant

Baseball fans love to watch home run hitters. Nothing in the game is more exciting than seeing a player belt the ball out of the park. By the start of the 1997 season, Mark McGwire had become one of the greatest long-ball hitters in baseball history.

Big Mac, as he'd been nicknamed by fans and sports journalists, didn't just hit a lot of homers. He hit *spectacular* homers; towering shots that soared right out of the stadium and seemed to rocket into orbit. Mark alone was worth the price of admission to an Oakland A's game. Fans showed up for batting practice hours in advance so they could watch him drill one ball after another into the stands.

The season got off to a good start. Mark was swinging the bat well and hitting a lot of home runs. Midway through, he was actually on pace to break Maris' record. But the second half of the season was difficult. Mark was tested both on and off the field.

First of all, Mark was trying to negotiate a new contract with the A's. His contract was set to expire at the end of the season. Unfortunately, the A's had a very expensive payroll and they knew they would not have enough money to pay Mark nearly what he was worth. So they faced a difficult decision. If they did not sign Mark to a new contract, he would become a free agent at the end of the year. He would be able to sign with any team he chose, and the A's would get nothing in return. But if the A's decided to trade Mark in the middle of the season, they would receive something of value in the deal.

Trade rumors swirled around Mark throughout the month of July. He tried to focus on baseball, but it was difficult. He was terribly distracted. Mark liked playing in Oakland. He liked the fact that it wasn't too far from Los Angeles, where Matt lived. The A's were the only team he had ever played for, and Mark really wasn't looking forward to changing uniforms.

As Mark waited for a decision to be made, his

game deteriorated. He hit only 5 home runs in the entire month of July and fell far behind record pace. Finally, on July 31, Mark got a call from his agent. It was a good news/bad news call. He had been traded to the St. Louis Cardinals. The bad news was that Mark would have to leave the West Coast. The good news was that the Cardinals were now managed by Tony La Russa — the man who'd been Mark's coach in Oakland and who had believed so strongly in him.

Still, it took Mark time to adjust. He was not only on a new team, but in a new league (the Cardinals play in the National League) and a new stadium. He was facing new pitchers and new umpires. "It's all a question of feeling comfortable," Mark said. And for a while he wasn't. Mark had hit 34 home runs with the A's. He had averaged 1 home run in every 10 at bats. But he hit just one homer in his first ten *days* with the Cardinals.

Eventually Mark adjusted to his new surroundings. He hit 8 more home runs in August and 11 in the first three weeks of September. With seven games to play, Mark had 54 home runs. To catch Maris — there it was again! — he would have had to hit 1 home run in each game. That didn't happen, but Mark came close enough to give baseball fans quite a thrill. He finished the season with 58 home runs. He became only the second player in history to hit 50 or more homers in consecutive seasons. The other player was Babe Ruth.

"Mark Is a Better Person Than He Is a Player"

By the end of that season, Mark had fallen in love with St. Louis. The fans adored him and made him feel right at home. It helped that Mark's son liked St. Louis, too. Matt visited his father shortly after Mark was traded and gave the city — and the team — his stamp of approval. That was all Mark needed to hear.

On September 16, Mark happily signed a new three-year contract with the Cardinals. The deal was worth more than $9 million a year. That's a lot of money, of course. But Mark could have gotten even more if he had shopped around. He just wasn't interested. Mark has never been a greedy athlete. Although he has had many offers, he's turned down just about every endorsement opportunity that has come his way. Mark doesn't even have an athletic shoe deal!

"Too distracting," he has explained of his reasoning.

So instead of driving a hard bargain, Mark simply signed with the Cardinals. He did insist that one unusual clause be written into the contract: His son would be guaranteed a seat on all of the team's flights. That way, Matt could be a Cardinals batboy and spend even more time with his dad.

Mark started earning his money that very evening by hitting a 517-foot home run. It was the longest shot in the history of Busch Stadium. His real value, though, was obvious before he even took the field. At a news conference to announce the new contract, a reporter asked Mark about his interest in helping children. This had been a subject close to Mark's heart for a long time. He had become truly passionate about it when he began dating a woman who volunteered at a shelter for abused children near Los Angeles. Mark was overwhelmed by what he saw there. He admired the spirit of the kids that he met. But he also felt sorry for them — and he wanted to help.

Mark talked to his girlfriend about donating money to the shelter. He even suggested the possibility of starting his own foundation to benefit abused children. At first, he wasn't sure how to translate his words and thoughts into action. He just wanted to do something to make their lives better.

By the time he signed his new contract, he had formulated a plan. He would donate one million dollars a year for the next three years to the Mark McGwire Foundation for Children.

The organization's sole purpose was to help needy and abused children. When Mark made this announcement at the news conference, he broke down and cried. The sight of this gentle giant weeping touched the hearts of people all over the nation. Everyone knew Mark McGwire was one of the strongest men in baseball. They didn't know he was also one of the kindest. As manager Tony La Russa said, "Mark is a better person than he is a player."

And that's saying a lot.

"I just want people to realize that I'm not *just* a baseball player," Mark told *The Sporting News*. "I'm a human being, like everybody else. I would rather be known for what I'm doing for my foundation than as a baseball player. It means a lot to me."

Mark's work did not go unrecognized. In an era when many professional athletes prefer *not* to be role models, Mark has embraced that responsibility. In December 1997 he was named Sportsman of the Year by *The Sporting News*, mainly because of his actions *off* the field. "I hope this award helps people understand I am more than an athlete," Mark said. "It's what I do, but it's not who I am."

7

The Great Home Run Race

Many people believe that 1998 will be remembered as one of the greatest seasons
in baseball. It was a year in which the New York
Yankees challenged a ninety-two-year-old record
for most victories in a season. It was a year in
which twenty-year-old Kerry Wood of the
Chicago Cubs struck out twenty batters in a single game! It was a year in which Cal Ripken,
baseball's record holder for "most consecutive
games played," purposely ended his streak.
Many records were threatened or broken; fans
got excited about the game all over again.

But what really captured everyone's attention
was the Great Home Run Race. Mark McGwire

had come within a breath of Roger Maris' single-season record one year earlier. Now he was healthy and happy and poised to break the record. But Mark wasn't the only one chasing Roger. He would be challenged by the sensational Seattle Mariners outfielder, Ken Griffey, Jr. Ken was smaller and leaner than Mark, but he knew how to hit home runs. He would push Mark. Together they would go after the record.

Mark jumped out to an early lead, hitting home runs in his first four games. By June 1 he had hit 27 homers. One was a 545-foot blast that broke his own Busch Stadium record. Griffey kept pace with Mark, but, as it turned out, they weren't alone in the quest. Soon the pair was joined by a third slugger: Sammy Sosa.

Mark played very well in June. He hit 10 home runs. But Sammy was incredible. He went on a tear, hitting 20 homers in a single *month*! Suddenly, it was very much a three-way competition. At the All-Star break, in the first week of July, Mark had 37 home runs. That tied Reggie Jackson's all-time record for most home runs in the first half of a season. Mark was actually ahead of Roger Maris' record pace. He was followed closely by Ken Griffey, who had 35 home runs, and Sammy Sosa, who had 33.

Feeling the Pressure

There were times during the season when Mark seemed to wilt in the spotlight. He tried to be gracious and accommodating with the media and with fans. But his innate shyness had never left him, and sometimes the unrelenting publicity was just too much to bear. There were times when he would finish a game and find more than 100 reporters waiting by his locker. Every day he was asked the same question: *"Will you break the record?"*

Sometimes Mark appeared grumpy during interviews. He snapped at reporters. On one occasion he said, "You guys are making too big a deal out of this!" People began to wonder whether he could handle the pressure of trying to break the home run record. Their concern was legitimate. Thirty-seven years earlier, Roger Maris had trouble coping with the media attention that came with trying to break Babe Ruth's single-season home run record. In fact, Maris had become so nervous and tense that his hair began falling out in clumps!

Mark's thick red hair remained in place, but his patience was wearing thin. At one point he said he felt like a "caged animal." What stung Mark most was a story that was first reported in the middle of August. Mark was criticized for using a substance known as androstenedione as part of his training program.

Androstenedione (pronounced an-dro-steen-*dy*-own) is a natural food supplement that allows an athlete to train harder and get stronger. Although its long-term effects are not known and therefore it should *not* be taken by children or teenagers, it *is* legal and can be purchased without a doctor's prescription. Its use is banned by some athletic organizations, including the National Football League, the National Collegiate Athletic Association, and the International Olympic Committee. But it has not been banned by Major League Baseball or the National Basketball Association. Bottom line: Mark was not breaking any rules.

Loosening Up

Most people didn't realize that Mark wasn't really angry at the press. The controversy aside, he was actually concerned that he wasn't *interesting* enough. So he called a few of his friends who were stand-up comics. He asked them to suggest jokes he could use when being interviewed. He also studied baseball history so that he could talk intelligently about the careers of Maris and Ruth.

There was one other thing Mark did: He watched Sammy Sosa. Sammy seemed to be having fun with the home run race. What a concept! The Chicago Cubs' outfielder enjoyed the media attention. He smiled a lot. He joked with reporters and fans. And he constantly praised his rival, Mark McGwire. So began a great friendship. Sammy and Mark supported each other in their pursuit of the record.

Even better, Mark learned how to have a good time.

"I listened to a bunch of my friends, and they were all saying 'Just have fun,'" Mark related, "so I decided that I was going to enjoy this."

On August 20, before a doubleheader against the New York Mets, Mark sat down at a podium and gracefully handled a crowd of more than two hundred members of the media. He answered all of the questions and even told a few jokes. He seemed to be a new man. A short while later, Mark went out and hit his 50th and 51st home runs. By doing so, he set another record. He became the first player in history to hit 50 homers in three consecutive seasons.

After hitting number 50, Mark did something he hadn't done all year: He pumped his fist in the air and waved to the crowd. After the game, he explained the celebration. "When I got to fifty-eight [homers] at the finish of last season, I thought it was possible to get the record. But one of my goals going into spring training was to get fifty again, because I knew that was reachable. The rest of it is icing on the cake. I'm just going to do my best."

Mark had always said that anyone hoping to break Maris' record would have to have at least 50 home runs heading into September, the final month of the season. He hit number 55 on August 30. Sammy Sosa hit his 55th one day later. Ken Griffey was now 8 home runs behind and slowing down. But the long-standing record was clearly in jeopardy.

All over the country, people were talking about the Great Home Run Race, even people who usually didn't care about baseball. Whenever the Cardinals came to town, games were sold out. And the strangest thing began to happen: Fans sometimes rooted *against* their own team. If the pitcher for the home team didn't give Mark good pitches to hit, that pitcher would be booed. Everyone wanted to see Mark hit a home run. They wanted to see him break the record.

They wanted to be part of history.

8

Record Breaker!

Like a true slugger, Mark jumped from 55 to 59 home runs with a staggering two-day display of power. On September 1 he hit 2 home runs in a 7–1 victory over the Florida Marlins. On September 2 he hit 2 more home runs off the Marlins. That barrage brought Mark to within striking distance of the immortal Babe Ruth, who had hit 60 homers in his finest season, 61 years earlier in 1927.

A lot of people rooted for Mark in the home run race because they felt he was a true home run hitter, much like Ruth was. Both men seemed bigger than life. They didn't just hit home runs. They punished baseballs. And, like

Babe, whose heart melted when he was around children, Mark was a superhero whose bulging muscles masked a gentle core.

By September it didn't matter that the Cardinals were far out of the National League pennant race. As long as Mark was playing, Cardinals fans had plenty to cheer about. So did everyone who cared about baseball. "I have run into fans on the street who said they hated the game of baseball because of what we did to it [during the 1994 strike]," Mark said. "And it's because of what I am doing and Sammy's doing and other great players that the fans are coming back. All I can say is thank you."

All eyes were on Busch Stadium on September 5, when Mark became only the third player in history to hit 60 home runs in a season. He drilled a fastball off Cincinnati Reds pitcher Dennis Reyes into the outfield stands in the first inning, setting off a wild celebration and a scramble for the historic ball. All of the baseballs pitched to Mark in the last few weeks of the season were dipped in a special invisible ink that glowed under infrared light. That way, league officials would find it easier to retrieve the right ball.

There was some concern that a fan might catch one of Mark's record-breaking home runs and demand a lot of money before returning it. There is a huge market for sports memorabilia, especially for items that are destined to wind up in the Baseball Hall of Fame in Cooperstown, New York. But the man who caught Mark's 60th homer asked for very little in return. He traded the ball in exchange for an autographed cap and bat, and a chance to take batting practice with the Cardinals.

A Great Birthday Present

On the night of September 6, Mark had dinner with his family. The next day was his father's birthday. John McGwire was about to turn sixty-one years old. Mark thought it would be terrific if he could hit his 61st home run on his dad's sixty-first birthday. To tie Roger Maris' record — that would be the greatest present in the world.

On Monday afternoon, September 7, the Cardinals hosted the Chicago Cubs. The scene was set for a perfect conclusion to the home run race. Sammy had 58 home runs, Mark had 60. It seemed appropriate that they should be on the field together when the record could be tied or broken. It also was appropriate that the family of Roger Maris had flown to St. Louis for the game. Maris had died of cancer in 1985, and his wife was suffering from a heart condition. But the six Maris children were all in the stands. As the game began, there was only one important person missing: Mark's son.

Matthew arrived from California just a few minutes before the start of the game. He quickly changed into his Cardinals uniform and ran out to the dugout, where he met his father. Matt gave his dad a good luck kiss just before Mark headed to the on-deck circle. A few minutes later, at 1:22 P.M., Mark jumped on Mike Morgan's third pitch and pulled the ball deep to left field. For a moment it looked as though the ball might sail foul . . . but it didn't. As Mark raised his fists in celebration, the ball curled just inside the foul pole. The crowd went wild!

Number 61!

As Mark rounded the bases, the Maris family stood and applauded. In right field, Sammy Sosa smiled and clapped one hand into his mitt. After rounding the bases, Mark hugged his son. Then he touched his chest with a fingertip and looked up at the sky. "I wanted the Maris family to know that Roger was with me," he later explained. Finally, Mark pointed toward his father in the stands and smiled.

"Happy birthday, Dad!" he shouted.

The Shot Heard Round the World

The bat that Maris used to hit his 61st homer was flown from Cooperstown to St. Louis for the Cardinals' series against the Cubs. On Tuesday, September 8, before he took the field, Mark held the bat in his hands and rubbed it lovingly against his chest, like a good luck charm.

"Roger," he whispered, "I hope you're with me tonight."

Everyone was with Mark on this historic night. The game was broadcast live on the FOX TV network and received the highest rating of any regular-season game since 1982. Busch Stadium was filled to capacity. Signs were draped all over the stadium, imploring Mark to break the record.

In his first at bat Mark appeared nervous. He swung on a 3–0 pitch from Steve Trachsel (something Mark almost never does) and grounded out. In the fourth inning, as Mark came to the plate, the crowd stood and applauded. This time Mark didn't wait. He attacked the first pitch from Trachsel and sent a screaming line drive down the left-field line. The crowd held its breath. At first the ball looked like it would fall into the corner for an extra-base hit . . . but it didn't. It hung in the air *just long enough* and dipped over the fence.

"I'll tell you what, I was so shocked because I didn't think the ball had enough to go out," Mark later said. "It's an absolutely incredible feeling."

At 341 feet it was the shortest home run Mark had hit all season. But it was easily the most important, for *this* was number **62!** Mark McGwire was the new home run king!

Busch Stadium erupted when the ball disappeared over the fence. Mark was so excited that he threw his arms into the air and ran right past first base without touching it. Cardinals first-base coach Dave McKay grabbed Mark's hands, congratulated him, and pulled him back to the base. Then Mark went on with his delirious home run trot. Each of the Cubs infielders shook his hand. Catcher Scott Servais extended his hand as Mark crossed the plate, but that wasn't nearly enough. Mark wrapped his arms around Servais and gave him a big bear hug.

"I just hope I didn't act foolish," Mark said. "This is history."

No one thought he was foolish. Mark's display of emotion captivated the nation. After he rounded the bases, Mark was greeted by his son. He picked Matt up and held him high in the air. Then he was mobbed by his teammates. As the celebration roared on — the game was stopped for eleven minutes — Sammy Sosa jogged in from right field and embraced Mark. The two greatest sluggers in the game hugged each other for several moments. Then they shared a high five.

"When he hugged me, it was a great moment," Sammy said. "I could see the emotion in Mark's eyes. This is a great moment for baseball, and everybody knows that. It's something I'm not going to forget."

Neither will the Maris family. In the most poignant moment of the evening, Mark bounded into the stands to hug and kiss the children of the man whose record he had broken. Then he grabbed a microphone and addressed the stadium crowd. In a raspy voice choked with emotion, Mark said, "To all my family, my son, the Cubs, Sammy Sosa. It's unbelievable. Thank you, St. Louis!"

Home run ball number 62 was retrieved by Tim Forneris, a twenty-two-year-old Busch Stadium groundskeeper. Some people estimated that the ball could be sold to collectors for as much as two million dollars. But Forneris simply returned it Mark. "It's not mine to begin with," Forneris said graciously. "McGwire just lost it and I brought it home."

In a few hours the ball — along with Mark's bat — was on its way to a new home: the Baseball Hall of Fame. It would be put on display for all the world to see, right beside the bat that Roger Maris had used to hit his 61st home run.

The Race Goes On

Meanwhile, the Great Home Run Race continued. After a long dry spell, Sammy Sosa hit 4 homers in three days to catch Mark. His 62nd home run came on September 13 at Chicago's Wrigley Field. Mark regained the lead on September 15, but Sammy hit a grand slam the next day to tie the race at 63.

Two days later, Mark took the lead again. He hit a 3–1 pitch from Milwaukee's Rafael Roque 417 feet into the left-center-field bleachers at County Stadium. After hitting number 64, Mark seemed amazed at his own accomplishment — and at the accomplishment of Sammy Sosa. "What we've done in the game of baseball, nobody's ever done," Mark said. "We're both rooting for each other, and wherever the numbers finish, where we land, that's the way it is."

Mark's 65th home run landed in the bleachers at Milwaukee's County Stadium. It came on Sunday, September 20, in the first inning of an 11–6 victory over the Brewers.

Mark appeared to have hit another homer in the fifth inning. He lofted a long fly ball to center field. As the ball dropped from the sky, a fan sitting in the first row of the bleachers reached out over a railing and caught it. Umpire Bob Davidson ruled that the fan had leaned into the field of play and interfered with the ball. He waved off the home run and awarded Mark a ground-rule double.

"It looked like it was a home run," Mark said after the game. But he really wasn't upset. In fact, he went on to hit five *more* home runs in the final three days of the season, all against the Montreal Expos. On September 25, he blasted number 66 — only forty-five minutes after Sammy Sosa hit *his* 66th.

Sammy stayed pat, but Mark wasn't quite done. The following day, he connected with numbers 67 and 68. It wasn't until the final day of the regular season, Sunday, September 27, that Mark McGwire ended his historic streak with a punctuation mark — or two!! — exclamations, that is.

Mark McGwire would finish the season with 70 home runs, more than any other player in the history of baseball.

"It's unheard of," Mark marveled. "I'm in awe of myself right now. I think [the record] is going to stand for a while." That's putting it modestly. Most people wonder if it can ever be done again.

Yet, in spite of his crowning achievement, it was number 65 that was perhaps the most special of all. Mark revealed that *before* the 1998 season had even begun, he had a little chat with his son. He asked Matt how many home runs he'd like Dad to hit.

Matt thought about it for a moment. Then he looked his father in the eye and suggested a big number. A number so large that no one had ever come close to it before. A record-breaking number.

"Sixty-five," Matt said.

At the time, it may have seemed like wishful thinking. But home run heroes have a way of making wishes come true. And sometimes, so do fathers.

#25 MARK McGWIRE

St. Louis Cardinals — First Base • Bats: Right • Throws: Right
Height: 6'5" • Weight: 250 • Born: October 1, 1963

YEAR	TEAM	AVG.	GAMES	AT BATS	RUNS	HITS	2B	3B	HR	RBI	BB	SO
1986	A's	.189	18	53	10	10	1	0	3	9	4	18
1987	A's	.289	151	557	97	161	28	4	49	118	71	131
1988	A's	.260	155	550	87	143	22	1	32	99	76	117
1989	A's	.231	143	490	74	113	17	0	33	95	83	94
1990	A's	.235	156	523	87	123	16	0	39	108	110	116
1991	A's	.201	154	483	62	97	22	0	22	75	93	116
1992	A's	.268	139	467	87	125	22	0	42	104	90	105
1993	A's	.333	27	84	16	28	6	0	9	24	21	19
1994	A's	.252	47	135	26	34	3	0	9	25	37	40
1995	A's	.274	104	317	75	87	13	0	39	90	88	77
1996	A's	.312	130	423	104	132	21	0	52	113	116	112
1997	A's	.284	105	366	48	104	24	0	34	81	58	98
1997	Cards	.253	51	174	38	44	3	0	24	42	43	61
1998	Cards	.299	155	509	130	152	21	0	70	147	162	155
Total		.264	1535	5131	941	1353	219	5	457	1130	1052	1259

McGWIRE'S HOME RUN CHART

#	GM	DATE	PITCHER, CLUB	H/A	INN.	OB	DIST.
1	1	Mar.31	R. Martinez, L.A.	H	5	3	364'
2	2	Apr. 2	F. Lankford, L.A.	H	12	2	368'
3	3	Apr. 3	M. Langston, S.D.	H	5	1	364'
4	4	Apr. 4	D. Wengert, S.D.	H	6	2	419'
5	13	Apr. 14	J. Suppan, Ari.	H	3	1	424'
6	13	Apr. 14	J. Suppan, Ari.	H	5	0	347'
7	13	Apr. 14	B. Manuel, Ari.	H	8	1	462'
8	16	Apr. 17	M. Whiteside, Phi.	H	4	1	419'
9	19	Apr. 21	T. Moore, Mon.	A	3	1	437'
10	23	Apr. 25	J. Spradlin, Phi.	A	7	1	419'
11	27	Apr. 30	M. Pisciotta, Chi. (N)	A	8	1	371'
12	28	May 1	R. Beck, Chi. (N)	A	9	1	362'
13	34	May 8	R. Reed, N.Y. (N)	A	3	1	358'
14	36	May 12	P. Wagner, Mil.	H	5	2	527'
15	38	May14	K. Millwood, Atl.	H	4	0	381'
16	40	May 16	L. Hernández, Fla.	H	4	0	545'
17	42	May 18	J. Sanchez, Fla.	H	4	0	478'
18	43	May 19	T. Green, Phi.	A	3	1	440'
19	43	May 19	T. Green, Phi.	A	5	1	471'
20	43	May 19	W. Gomes, Phi.	A	8	1	451'
21	46	May 22	M. Gardner, S.F.	H	6	1	425'
22	47	May 23	R. Rodriguez, S.F.	H	4	0	366'
23	47	May 23	J. Johnstone, S.F.	H	5	2	477'
24	48	May 24	R. Nen, S.F.	H	12	1	397'
25	49	May 25	J. Thomson, Col.	H	1	0	433'
26	52	May 29	D. Miceli, S.D.	A	9	1	388'
27	53	May 30	A. Ashby, S.D.	A	1	0	423'
28	59	June 5	O. Hershiser, S.F.	H	1	1	409'
29	62	June 8	J. Bere, Chi. (A)	A	4	1	356'
30	64	June 10	J. Parque, Chi. (A)	A	3	2	409'
31	65	June 12	A. Benes, Ari.	A	3	3	438'

#	GM	DATE	PITCHER, CLUB	H/A	INN.	OB	DIST.
32	69	June 17	J. Lima, Hou.	A	3	0	347'
33	70	June 18	S. Reynolds, Hou.	A	5	0	449'
34	76	June 24	J. Wright, Cle.	A	4	0	433'
35	77	June 25	D. Burba, Cle.	A	1	0	461'
36	79	June 27	M. Trombley, Minn.	A	7	1	431'
37	81	June 30	G. Rusch, K.C.	H	7	0	472'
38	89	July 11	B. Wagner, Hou.	H	11	1	485'
39	90	July 12	S. Bergman, Hou.	H	1	0	405'
40	90	July 12	S. Elarton, Hou.	H	7	0	415'
41	95	July 17	B. Bohanon, L.A.	H	1	0	511'
42	95	July 17	A. Osuna, L.A.	H	8	0	425'
43	98	July 20	B. Boehringer, S.D.	A	5	1	458'
44	104	July 26	J. Thomson, Col.	A	4	0	452'
45	105	July 28	M. Myers, Mil.	H	8	0	408'
46	115	Aug. 8	M. Clark, Chi.(N)	H	4	0	374'
47	118	Aug. 11	B. Jones, N.Y. (N)	H	4	0	464'
48	124	Aug. 19	M. Karchner, Chi.(N)	A	8	0	430'
49	124	Aug. 19	T. Mulholland,Chi.(N)	A	10	0	402'
50	125	Aug. 20	W. Blair, N.Y. (N)	A	7	0	369'
51	126	Aug. 20	R. Reed, N.Y. (N)	A	1	0	385'
52	129	Aug. 22	F. Cordova, Pitt.	A	1	0	477'
53	130	Aug. 23	R. Rincon, Pitt.	A	8	0	393'
54	132	Aug. 26	J. Speier, Fla.	H	8	1	509'
55	136	Aug. 30	D. Martinez, Atl.	H	7	2	501'
56	138	Sept. 1	L. Hernandez, Fla.	A	7	0	450'
57	138	Sept. 1	D. Pall, Fla.	A	9	0	472'
58	139	Sept. 2	B. Edmonson, Fla.	A	7	1	497'
59	139	Sept. 2	R. Stanifer, Fla.	A	8	1	458'
60	141	Sept. 5	D. Reyes, Cin.	H	1	1	381'
61	143	Sept. 7	M. Morgan, Chi. (N)	H	1	0	430'
62	144	Sept. 8	S. Trachsel, Chi. (N)	H	4	0	341'

#	GM	DATE	PITCHER, CLUB	H/A	INN.	OB	DIST.
63	151	Sept. 15	J. Christiansen, Pit.	H	9	0	385'
64	155	Sept. 18	R. Roque, Mil.	A	4	1	417'
65	157	Sept. 20	S. Karl, Mil.	A	1	1	423'
66	161	Sept. 25	S. Bennett, Mon.	H	5	2	375'
67	162	Sept. 26	D. Hermanson, Mon.	H	4	0	403'
68	162	Sept. 26	K. Bullinger, Mon.	H	7	1	435'
69	163	Sept. 27	M. Thurman, Mon.	H	3	0	377'
70	163	Sept. 27	C. Pavano, Mon.	H	7	2	371'

September 8, 1998.
Big Mac blasts his way into home run history, breaking
Roger Maris' single season record with home run number
62.

"This is history"—Mark McGwire after hitting 62nd homer.

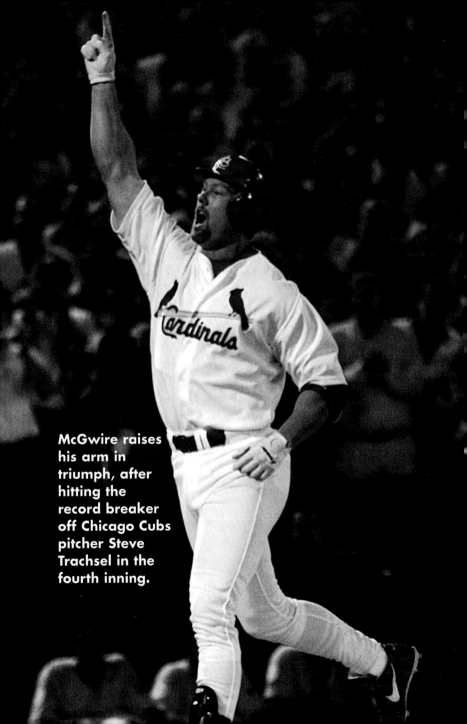

McGwire raises his arm in triumph, after hitting the record breaker off Chicago Cubs pitcher Steve Trachsel in the fourth inning.

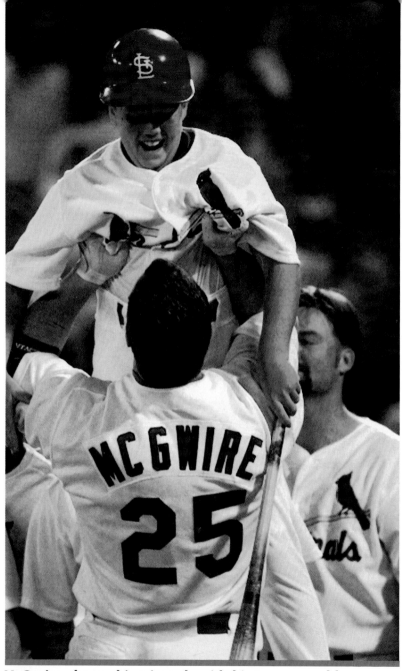

McGwire shares his triumph with his ten-year-old son Matthew, the Cardinal's bat boy.

The Chicago Cubs Sammy Sosa runs in from the outfield to congratulate McGwire. The real race for the record is just beginning.

Mark McGwire doesn't disappoint. On the field and off, he delivers for his fans.

It's going...going...gone!
Big Mac does it again.
He ends the season with
70 homers!

Sosa and McGwire joke around before a game—partners and friends in the greatest home run derby of all time.

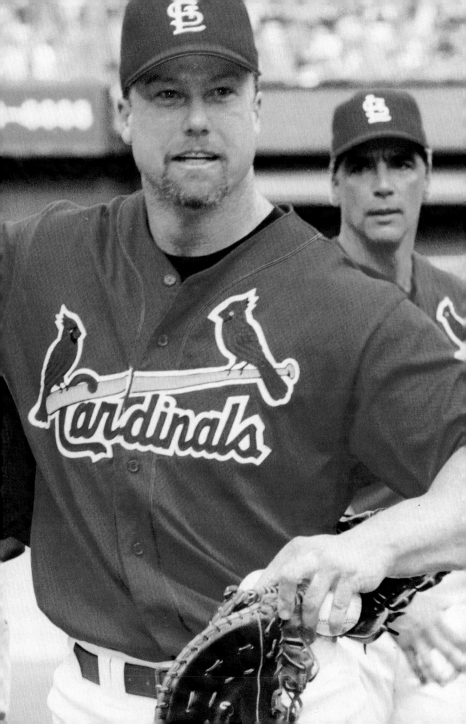

HOME RUN HERO!

Sammy Sosa

HOME RUN HERO!

Sammy Sosa

BY JOE LAYDEN

SCHOLASTIC INC.
New York Toronto London Auckland Sydney
Mexico City New Delhi Hong Kong

About the Author

Joe Layden has written nearly two dozen books for children and adults, including titles such as *NBA Game Day, Against the Odds, The Kobe Bryant Story,* and *Dribble, Shoot, Score!* He is also the author of *Women in Sports: The Complete Book on the World's Greatest Female Athletes, The Art of Magic,* and *America on Wheels.* Mr. Layden frequently visits school classrooms to discuss the craft of writing with students. He lives in upstate New York with his wife, Susan, and their daughter, Emily.

Photography credits: Mark McGwire cover: Jed Jacobsohn/Allsport. Sammy Sosa cover: Elsa Hasch/Allsport. Page 1: David Klutho/Sports Illustrated/Time Inc.; page 2 Rich Pilling/MLB Photos; page 3: Eric Draper/AP/Wide World; page 4: Ed Reinke/AP Photo/Wide World; page 5: Green/Sports Illustrated/Time Inc.; page 6: Tom Di-Pace/Sports Illustrated/Time Inc.; page 7: Gary Dineen/AP/Wide World; pages 8-9: Reuters/Tim Parker/Archive; page 10: Jed Jacobsohn/Allsport; page 11: Kent Horner/AP/Wide World; page 12: Matthew Stockman/Allsport; page 13: Reuters/Scott Olson/Archive Photos; page 14: David Durochik/MLB Photos; page 14 inset: Elsa Hasch/Allsport; page 15 Matthew Stockman/Allsport; page 16: Stephen Green/MLB Photos.

If you purchased this book without a cover, you should be aware that this book is stolen property. It was reported as "unsold and destroyed" to the publisher, and neither the author nor the publisher has received any payment for this "stripped book."

No part of this publication may be reproduced in whole or in part, or stored in a retrieval system, or transmitted in any form or by any means, electronic, mechanical, photocopying, recording, or otherwise, without written permission of the publisher. For information regarding permission, write to Scholastic Inc., Attention: Permissions Department, 555 Broadway, New York, NY 10012.

ISBN 0-439-05746-9

Copyright © 1999 by Scholastic Inc.
All rights reserved. Published by Scholastic Inc.
SCHOLASTIC and associated logos are trademarks and/or registered trademarks of Scholastic Inc.

12 11 10 9   1 2 3 4/0

Printed in the U.S.A.

First Scholastic printing, January 1999

For Sam — A Little Slugger

HOME RUN HERO!

Sammy Sosa

1

Chasing History

September 13, 1998

The race was supposed to be over.
Just a few days earlier Mark McGwire
had taken control. The hulking first baseman
for the St. Louis Cardinals had blasted his 62nd
home run of the season. With that shot McGwire
had shattered one of the oldest and most prized
records in all of sports: the single-season record
for most home runs.

The record had been held by Roger Maris of
the New York Yankees, who hit 61 homers in
1961. For thirty-seven years the record had
stood. In fact, it had barely been threatened. But
in the summer of 1998, McGwire and Sammy

Sosa of the Chicago Cubs had led an all-out assault on Maris' magnificent record.

Mark and Sammy chased each other across the country and across six months of baseball. They hit home runs like no one had ever hit them before. They hit them in bunches and batches. They hit them farther, and with greater consistency, than anyone who had ever played the game.

Along the way, a funny thing happened. People fell in love with baseball all over again. Baseball is often called the great American pastime, because it is our oldest and most cherished sport. In the past few years, however, the love affair had been tested. It had grown stale. A labor dispute in 1994 had left many fans bitter and disinterested. Basketball and football captured new fans, while baseball slipped into the background. But in 1998 baseball moved back into the spotlight.

The athletes most responsible for this change were Mark McGwire and Sammy Sosa, two men from completely different backgrounds but with a shared passion for their sport. Their friendly rivalry captured the hearts of sports fans everywhere. As they sprinted toward the magical number — 62! — baseball enjoyed a popularity it hadn't known in years. Everyone followed the Great Home Run Race. As Bud Selig, the com-

4

missioner of Major League Baseball said, "We've been blessed."

Down to the Wire

Mark McGwire was the first to reach the historic number. With an incredible outburst in early September he had surpassed both the legendary Babe Ruth (who once hit 60 home runs in a season) and Maris. Mark had also pulled well ahead of Sammy. A lot of people thought the race might be over. After all, Sammy had downplayed the race all season. He was a big fan of Mark's and he seemed content to be runner-up.

"I want Mark to break the record," Sammy had told reporters earlier in the season. "He's the man. If he breaks it, I would like to break it and be in second."

Now Sammy was about to get his wish . . . and maybe just a little bit more.

On this Sunday afternoon, as he walked to the plate in the bottom of the ninth inning of a game against the Milwaukee Brewers, Sammy was only 1 home run behind Mark. He had already tied Maris' record with his 61st homer in the fifth inning. Now he was batting again.

There were 40,846 fans at Wrigley Field, the Cubs home stadium, the largest crowd of the

season. They stood and cheered wildly as Sammy stepped into the batter's box. Milwaukee pitcher Eric Plunk threw two balls and a strike. Sammy was trying to be patient. The Cubs were trailing by two runs. They were in the thick of a play-off race, and this game was not over. Sammy could help them stay alive.

Plunk went into his windup and hurled a fast-ball toward the plate. Sammy watched it carefully. It was perfect — right out over the middle of the plate. Sammy's bat connected with a tremendous *crack*! The ball sailed toward the left-field bleachers . . . and into the record books.

2

Field of Dreams

Samuel Peralta Sosa was born November 10, 1968, in San Pedro de Macoris, a city on the southeastern coast of the Dominican Republic. The Dominican Republic is a small, mountainous Latin American country in the Caribbean Sea. It borders Haiti on the west. Puerto Rico lies to its east. Most Dominicans are descendants of Spanish colonists and African slaves. The dominant language of the country is Spanish.

There is a great deal of poverty in the Dominican Republic, and Sammy often felt its sting when he was growing up. He is one of seven children. Sammy's father, Juan Montero,

died when Sammy was only seven years old. That left Sammy's mother, Lucrecya, with the burden of feeding and raising a huge family by herself.

Lucrecya worked as a cook. She prepared meals for workers in a nearby factory. The job was extremely demanding and left Lucrecya with little time for her children. And it didn't pay much money. There were many nights when Sammy had trouble falling asleep because of hunger pangs. It's no wonder that now, as a millionaire professional athlete in the United States, Sammy likes to say, "Every day is a holiday for me." Considering his background, it's almost a miracle that Sammy ever made it to the major leagues.

When he was very young, Sammy didn't even play sports. He was too busy trying to find ways to help support his family. That he is considered one of the hardest-working players in baseball, a man who does whatever he has to do in order to improve his game and be the best, is the result of the discipline and drive that he developed as a small boy.

Sammy's entire family shared a tiny, two-room apartment in a run-down building that once was a hospital. Sammy didn't even have a bed. He slept on an old, thin mattress that was thrown on the floor.

On most days, Sammy would rise early in the morning and rush out into the dusty streets of San Pedro de Macoris looking for an opportunity to make a few extra dollars. "I did anything I could that was honest," he once said.

Sometimes Sammy shined shoes for local businessmen. Each customer gave him 25 cents. When he was through shining shoes, Sammy would sell oranges for 10 cents apiece. He also washed cars. Sammy's dreams were small then. He wasn't thinking about fame and fortune. His only concern was helping to put food on his family's table.

As Sammy once told a reporter from the *Chicago Tribune*, "When I was back home a long time ago, when I was a shoeshine boy, I never thought I'd be in the major leagues. But I guess anything can happen."

A Way Out

In the United States, it's not unusual for kids who are raised in poverty to use sports as a way to escape their surroundings. Many aspiring professional basketball players come from depressed urban areas. They work hard to improve their skills in the hope that one day they can receive a college scholarship. A lucky few even

make it to the National Basketball Association, where the average salary is more than one million dollars!

In the Dominican Republic, the sport of choice is baseball. Just as many city kids in America begin dribbling when they're barely old enough to walk, kids in the Dominican Republic are practically born with baseball mitts on their hands. Dominicans are passionate about baseball. They're good at it, too. Children in the Dominican Republic learn the fundamentals of the sport at a young age. Many of them play every day. They dream of someday wearing the uniform of a major league team.

The odds are against them, of course. But it's not an impossible dream. In fact, San Pedro de Macoris has produced more Major League Baseball players, per capita, than any other city in the world! For example, big-leaguers Mariano Duncan, Julio Franco, José Offerman, and Joaquin Andujar all were born in San Pedro de Macoris.

Unlike many of his friends, Sammy did not begin playing organized baseball until he was a teenager. Prior to that, he'd simply been too busy. But once he was introduced to the game by his older brother, Luis, Sammy was hooked. He couldn't afford the right equipment. In fact, his first glove was a milk carton turned inside out.

10

Sammy wasn't discouraged, though. When he was on the baseball field, he was happy. He felt like he could do anything. Sammy was fast and tireless. He had a strong arm and a natural swing.

It wasn't long before Sammy began dreaming big. He looked around and didn't see anyone who could hit the ball farther. He didn't see anyone with a better arm. So if other kids could make it to the big time . . . why not him?

The Big Break

In the summer of 1985, a man named Amado Dinzey first caught a glimpse of Sammy. Dinzey was a scout for the Texas Rangers. After watching Sammy play, Dinzey was so impressed that he called his boss, Omar Minaya. Dinzey suggested that Minaya get on the next plane to the Dominican Republic.

This wasn't a problem for Minaya, since he had been born in the Dominican Republic. Minaya was a good baseball player who had become a coach and scout in the Rangers organization. He had the authority to offer Sammy a contract — *if* he liked what he saw.

Minaya met Sammy at a field in San Pedro de Macoris. Sammy had been living and training in

Santo Domingo, so he had to take a four-hour bus ride home. When Minaya first saw him, Sammy did not look like a big-league prospect. He wore a tattered baseball uniform. His shoes had holes in them. Sammy was sixteen years old. He was 5 feet 10 inches tall and weighed less than 150 pounds. The scout thought Sammy looked malnourished.

"That's where the Sammy Sosa miracle began," Minaya later told the New York *Daily News*. "At least I like to call it a miracle, because of how far he has come to all these home runs he is hitting. Mark McGwire, I'm sure he comes from a very nice high school. Sammy Sosa comes from that bus. But he got off that bus ready to hit."

In fact, Sammy was ready to do *whatever* was asked of him. He wanted to prove to the scout that he was capable of making it as a professional ballplayer. Minaya asked Sammy to run a few sprints. He asked Sammy to take batting practice and play defense.

Minaya did not think he was watching a future all-star that day in San Pedro de Macoris. Sammy's swing was a bit ragged, and he seemed to lack strength, perhaps because he was so thin. "Some of the balls he'd hit to the outfield, they'd run out of steam," Minaya told the *Daily News*. But the scout loved Sammy's attitude.

And he thought the kid had enough natural talent that he was probably worth pursuing.

"There was something inside him, a fire," Minaya recalled. "Right from the start you could see how aggressive he was."

The Rangers eventually offered Sammy a contract with a signing bonus of $3,500. By major league standards, that's not much money. But it was far more than Sammy had ever seen in his life. He accepted the offer and signed his first contract. Sammy Sosa was a professional baseball player!

Sammy was careful with his money. He bought himself just one thing: a bicycle. He gave the rest of the money to his mother, so that she could feed and clothe her children. A few months later Sammy packed his meager belongings and boarded a plane bound for the United States. He was to join the Rangers' Rookie League team in Florida. At the airport he kissed his mother good-bye. It was a difficult moment, full of both joy and sadness. Sammy was flying off to a new country to follow his dream. But he was barely seventeen years old, and he did not speak a word of English.

As she watched her son disappear, Lucrecya began to cry.

3

A Whole New Ballgame

Sammy Sosa is widely regarded as one of the nicest men in professional sports. He always has time to sign autographs and chat with fans. And he never seems to get upset. For a long time, even *losing* didn't seem to bother Sammy. Unfortunately, he also had a reputation for being more concerned with improving his own statistics and earning a fat paycheck than with helping his team win.

But people who said that didn't understand Sammy's background. They didn't realize just how poor he had been as a child. When Sammy came to the United States to play professional

baseball in 1986, he had one goal in mind: *take care of my family.* Nothing else mattered. And the quickest way to increase his value was to put up some big numbers. Sammy knew that if he had a good batting average and drove in a lot of runs, he would make more money. And if he made more money, his mother and his brothers and sisters would have a better life back in the Dominican Republic.

"You've got to understand something about Latin players when they're young — or really any player from low economic backgrounds," Omar Minaya explained during an interview with *Sports Illustrated.* "They know the only way to make money is by putting up offensive numbers [improving their own statistics]."

Sammy was not motivated by championships when he first became a professional baseball player. But that doesn't mean he wanted to fail. In fact, he craved success in a way that most players could only imagine. Davey Lopes was a coach with the Rangers when Sosa first came to the United States. Lopes was struck by Sammy's recklessness at the plate, but also by his ambition and his willingness to learn.

"Sammy has always been hungry," Lopes told the *New York Post.* "He was a wild swinger without much discipline, and it didn't look like he'd ever hit the breaking ball consistently. But even

then you could see how hungry he was, how much he wanted to be successful. He had this great desire you could feel."

Learning the Ropes

Because Sammy was so young when he signed with the Rangers, it took time for him to learn how to play the game properly. It also took some time for him to mature physically. And, of course, he had to adjust to a new culture.

"At the beginning it was a little hard for me because my English was not the way it is now," Sammy once said. "The first time in the United States was a lot different because I had to communicate with my teammates and the people around me. I was lucky because there were some Puerto Rican players who I hung out with. They helped me out a lot. This is the way I was able to understand the life here in the United States."

Sammy improved steadily as he progressed through the minor leagues. But it was a long time before he began to display the kind of power and consistency that made him a home run king.

In his first year with the Rangers organization, Sammy batted .275 and hit 4 home runs. He also led the Gulf Coast League in doubles

and total bases. The next year he was promoted to the Rangers Class-A team in Gastonia, where he hit 11 home runs and led the team in batting with a .279 average. In 1988 he led the Florida State League in triples.

Sammy found himself riding a roller coaster in 1989. He started the season with Class-AA in Tulsa before being promoted all the way to the majors. In twenty-five games with the Rangers, Sammy's batting average was only .238, so he was sent down to Class-AAA in Oklahoma City. Before the season ended, he was traded to the Chicago White Sox.

Sammy spent the next two years with the White Sox. At times he showed great promise. In 1990, for example, he had 70 runs batted in (RBIs) and 32 stolen bases. Unfortunately, he also struck out 150 times. In 1991, Sammy struggled badly. His batting average was only .203. The White Sox liked Sammy's talent and potential, but they were impatient for him to develop into a more well-rounded player. So, in the spring of 1992, the White Sox traded Sammy to their crosstown rivals, the Chicago Cubs.

At only twenty-three years old, Sammy Sosa was about to play for his *third* major league team. Few people in baseball thought he would ever become a great player, let alone one of the most prolific home runs hitters in history. "I said he'd strike out a lot, but that he'd play hard all

the time," Davey Lopes remembered telling his boss in Texas. "But nobody, and I mean nobody, could see this coming."

Sammy could. He had faith in himself, even when others doubted him.

At Home in Wrigley

The Cubs play their home games at Wrigley Field, which is one of the oldest and smallest stadiums in baseball. It's an ideal home for a power hitter, which is what Sammy soon became. In 1993, his first full season with the Cubs, Sammy had a very good year. He hit 33 home runs and drove in 93 runs. But the statistic that really impressed people was Sammy's 36 stolen bases. No one in Cubs history had ever stolen more than 30 bases and hit more than 30 home runs in a single season. Sammy was a rare player. At 6 feet, 200 pounds, he was big and strong enough to hit the ball a long way. But he also had exceptional speed. That combination of skills is unusual. It's found only in the very best athletes.

Still, there were a lot of things that Sammy didn't understand about baseball. He relied on natural ability more than anything else. He made mistakes in the field. He tried to steal when he

shouldn't. Sometimes this frustrated his teammates and coaches. In an interview with *Sports Illustrated*, Cubs first baseman Mark Grace recalled Sammy's early days in a Chicago uniform. "When he first got here, you could see he had great physical skills," Grace said. "But he was so raw. He didn't know the strategy of the game. He didn't understand the concept of hitting behind runners. He didn't understand the concept of hitting the cutoff man to keep a double play in order. So many little things he just didn't know."

Sammy and Mark Grace are now good friends. In fact, Mark is one of Sammy's biggest fans. Like a lot of Sammy's teammates, he simply wanted Sammy to get the most out of his talent. Looking back on his first few years with the Cubs, Sammy realized that he wasn't playing up to his potential.

"When I first came to this team, I was all over the place and made a lot of mistakes," he said. "But I learned from my mistakes. Now I'm trying to be a smarter player. I try to think about situations before they happen."

Over the next four seasons, Sammy became one of the most productive offensive players in Major League Baseball. He had 25 home runs and 70 RBIs in 1994, despite missing more than fifty games. In 1995 he had 36 homers and 119

RBIs. In 1996 he had 40 home runs and 100 RBIs. Sammy might have hit 50 home runs that year if he hadn't broken his hand in August. The injury forced him to miss the last month and a half of the season.

Sammy got off to a good start again in 1997, and the Cubs rewarded him with a huge contract extension midway through the season. The deal was worth $42.5 million over the course of the next four years. Sammy was now one of the richest men in baseball. Money would never be a problem for him, or his family again.

Some critics felt that Sammy hadn't really earned such a big contract. Sure, he was a pretty good hitter, but there were still weaknesses in his game. They pointed to the fact that he had made just one All-Star team in his career. Sammy gave them more ammunition in 1997. Although he hit 37 home runs and had 119 RBIs, he also led the National League in strike-outs and hit only .246 with runners in scoring position.

Worst of all, Sammy had done little to help make Chicago a better team. Cubs fans had been waiting a long time for a World Series championship (since 1908!), and Sammy didn't seem like a player who was going to end that dry spell. *He* became a millionaire in 1997, but the *Cubs* had another dismal season. They won just sixty-eight games and lost ninety-four.

But the Cubs' management believed in Sammy. He was only twenty-eight years old, and he seemed to be improving with each season. He had rarely been injured, and he had a good attitude. "The one important variable was Sammy's maturity as a player," Cubs general manager Ed Lynch told *Sports Illustrated*. "We were banking that he would continue to improve."

Sammy was clearly a good investment. But even the Cubs could not have anticipated the leap he was about to make.

4

Homework

Like all great athletes, Sammy Sosa knows that true success does not happen by accident. For the first ten years of his Major League Baseball career, he relied primarily on talent. He was blessed with speed and strength. He had a cannon for a right arm. His skill at the plate and in the field had made him rich and famous.

But somewhere along the way, he wanted more. Now he wanted to help the Cubs win a pennant. And he wanted to prove that he was more than just a good baseball player. Sammy wanted to be one of the very best. The only way to achieve those goals was to go back to work. Sammy decided he would train harder during

the off-season than he had ever trained before. He would lift weights and jog. He would take endless hours of batting practice. He would shag fly balls in the outfield until his arm felt it like it was going to fall off.

That wasn't all. Sammy would also be going to school. After so many years of relying strictly on instinct, it was time for him to become a student of the game. "I wanted to get myself under control," Sammy explained.

The first step toward self-improvement was humility. Sammy had to understand that he wasn't the best player in baseball. He had to realize that there were other players from whom he could learn a thing or two. And he had to seek help.

Sammy approached Jeff Pentland, the Cubs' hitting coach. In previous years Sammy and Pentland had barely even spoken. Sammy hadn't believed he needed any help, and Pentland wanted to spend time with players who were willing to work with him. When Sammy came to Pentland, the coach was surprised. But he was also eager to help.

"I always thought this guy could really put up some gigantic numbers," Pentland told *Time* magazine. "But we had to get him to swing at better pitches and get him to be more patient."

Pentland gave Sammy a videotape to study over the winter. The tape included batting footage

of three players: Sammy, Mark Grace, and Chipper Jones of the Atlanta Braves. All three players had something in common. They tapped a foot on the ground as the pitch hurtled toward the plate. It was an unconscious way of triggering their hitting stroke. As Sammy watched, though, he noticed a subtle difference. Jones and Grace each tapped their foot as soon as the ball left the pitcher's hand. But Sammy waited until the last moment. While their swings were smooth and measured, Sammy's was wild. He was flailing at the ball. Only his remarkable hand speed prevented him from striking out even more than he did.

Sammy spent the winter at his home in the Dominican Republic. He worked for hours each day to improve his timing and discipline. He changed his tap step so that he had more time to swing at pitches. He began to feel more comfortable and confident at the plate.

Sammy talked with Pentland a lot during the winter. Together they began compiling a list of personal goals for the upcoming season. Oddly enough, "hitting sixty home runs" wasn't on the list. Sammy was much more concerned with raising his batting average above the .300 mark. If he did that, everything else would fall into place. The Cubs would win more games, and Sammy would have a better year.

"There was too much pressure last year," Sammy told *Sports Illustrated*. "Pressure from the contract, pressure to do it all. I felt if I didn't hit a home run, we wouldn't win. I was trying to hit two home runs in one at bat. Now I don't feel that anymore."

Sammy's teammates were quick to spot the changes. He showed up at spring training with the same relaxed attitude. He smiled and talked a lot. He joked with fans. But at the plate . . . Sammy was a different person. He was smarter, quicker. Instead of trying to pull every pitch into the left-field bleachers, he sprayed balls all over the place. He hit singles, doubles, triples — and home runs. In the past, opposing pitchers could always count on Sammy to jump on almost anything that crossed the plate. Not anymore. Now he watched and waited. In just a few short months he had become a far more mature — and dangerous — hitter.

"He realized you don't have to hit the first pitch . . . out of the ballpark," Mark Grace said. "There's nothing wrong with hitting the fourth pitch out of the park."

As Sammy put it, "I'm not scared to take a walk. If they walk me, I will go happy to first base." Sammy was growing as a hitter. He understood that walks were directly related to home runs. If a pitcher falls behind on the

25

count, he's going to try very hard to put the ball over the plate. And if the ball is over the plate, it's a lot easier to hit.

Sammy and Roger

Before the 1998 season began, there was a lot of talk about the possibility of someone breaking one of the most revered records in all of sports: the single-season mark for home runs. Mark McGwire of the St. Louis Cardinals had come close in 1997. He had hit 58, just three short of the record set by Roger Maris in the 1961 season.

McGwire was a big (6 feet 5 inches, 250 pounds), powerful man with 20-inch biceps and a flaming red goatee. He hit thunderous home runs that were known to do serious damage to stadium scoreboards. McGwire reminded baseball fans of Babe Ruth, the great New York Yankees slugger. Ruth hit 60 home runs in 1927, and his record had stood for thirty-four years.

Like the Babe, McGwire was a pure home run hitter. Whenever he stepped to the plate, fans held their breath in anticipation. He turned batting practice into a carnival, with fans gathering in the outfield bleachers to watch his towering shots.

Although many people pointed out the similarities between Ruth and McGwire, hardly *anyone* noticed that Sammy Sosa's career was strikingly similar to that of Roger Maris. Heading into the 1998 season, Sammy did not look like a player who was about to be part of the Great Home Run Race. And in the spring of 1961, Roger Maris was merely a better-than-average baseball player.

Look at the numbers. Sammy's career batting average prior to 1998 was .257. Maris' career average was .258. Sammy's single-season high for home runs was 40. Maris had never hit more than 39 homers in a season. Sammy had averaged 1 home run every 19.4 at bats. Maris had averaged 1 home run every 19.3 at bats. And there's more. Both players were 6 feet tall and weighed 200 pounds. Both were strong-armed right fielders. Both had been traded twice.

And both came out of nowhere to ignite a race into the record books.

The story of Roger Maris is both sad and heroic. He played for the Yankees in 1961. But most people did not want Maris to break Ruth's record. The Babe was cherished by Yankee fans, and his record was considered sacred. If anyone was going to break Ruth's mark, it was supposed to be Maris' teammate, Mickey Mantle.

Maris and Mantle staged a dramatic battle throughout the summer of '61. But Mantle faded near the end of the season, leaving Maris to chase Ruth by himself. The pressure took its toll on Maris, who was a shy and private man. He had trouble handling the intense glare of the media spotlight. Sometimes he refused to conduct interviews. Sportswriters and columnists criticized Maris. They said he didn't deserve to break Ruth's record. Fans — even New York fans — frequently booed him. As the season wore on, the twenty-six-year-old Maris nearly crumbled. He was so nervous that his hair began to fall out.

But Maris was a remarkably tough man. He survived with his dignity intact. On the final day of the season he hit his 61st home run to break the record that "couldn't" be broken. He also had 142 RBIs and was named American League MVP.

Unfortunately, baseball did not give Maris the credit he deserved. Because he played in more games than Ruth (162 to 154), Maris' home run record carried the mark of an asterisk for many years in all of baseball's record books. He died of cancer in 1985 and has yet to be inducted into the Baseball Hall of Fame.

When the 1997 season began, many people expected Mark McGwire to challenge the home run record. They expected a thrilling race

that might also include Ken Griffey, Jr., the sensational young outfielder for the Seattle Mariners.

Sammy Sosa?

No one gave him a thought. Like Roger Maris, he was standing in the shadows, quietly preparing to make history.

5

Slammin' Sammy!

The Great Home Run Race began just as most observers thought it would — with Mark McGwire and Ken Griffey, Jr., sprinting to an early lead. McGwire was nothing short of sensational. He picked up right where he had left off the previous fall, hitting a grand slam in the Cardinals' season opener on March 31. He proceeded to hit home runs in each of the Cards' first four games. Clearly, Mark was ready to make a run at Roger Maris' record.

Griffey also homered in his opener. And he continued to pound the ball at a torrid pace throughout the first month of the season. As

April came to a close, McGwire and Griffey were tied with 11 home runs apiece.

Sammy got off to a slightly slower start. He hit 6 home runs in April and 7 more in May. At that pace, he would have finished the season with approximately 40 homers. But, his *batting* average had soared to .340! Sammy looked like he was going to have a great all-around year. Just not a slugger's year. He didn't seem capable of keeping up with McGwire, who hit his 27th home run on May 30. At that point Big Mac had more than twice as many home runs as Sammy. But things were about to change.

June was Sammy's month. For thirty days he put on a dazzling display of offensive power. Never before had anyone erupted quite so dramatically. There were 2 home runs in a game against the Florida Marlins on June 1. Then there was a home run on June 3. And then 4 home runs in four days, from June 5 through June 8. The Cubs won every one of those games, and suddenly Sammy had 20 home runs.

But even then he was reluctant to wear the crown of a home run king. When reporters asked Sammy if he might have a chance to break Maris' record, he shook his head and smiled. "No, no, no," Sammy said. "Mark McGwire is the man. Maybe tomorrow he'll be motivated by this and hit two or three."

That didn't happen. Mark continued on a steady pace. He hit 10 home runs in June to finish the month with 37. Griffey had 33. Sammy, meanwhile, was treating each game like batting practice. Balls were flying out of National League parks at a stunning rate. On June 15, in a 6–5 victory over the Milwaukee Brewers, Sammy hit 3 home runs in a single game! He hit 2 homers on June 19 and 2 more on June 20, including a 500-foot blast that even had his teammates shaking their heads in disbelief.

When the month came to a close, Sammy had a total of 33 home runs. His 20 homers in June shattered the major league record for most home runs in a month. No one else had even come close. Not even Babe Ruth or Roger Maris. With almost no warning, Sammy Sosa had become *Slammin' Sammy*! And he had done it by becoming more patient at the plate. Sammy was waiting for the right pitches now. He was forcing pitchers to work hard against him. If they wanted to walk him, he would let them. But if they made a mistake . . . Sammy pounced.

"It's not easy for a Latin [American] player to take one hundred walks," Sammy said in a June interview with *Sports Illustrated*. "If I knew seven years ago the stuff I know now — taking pitches, being more relaxed — I would have put up even better numbers. But people have to understand where you're coming from."

Sammy was referring, of course, to his impoverished childhood in the Dominican Republic. That was all a memory now. But it remained a vivid memory for Sammy. He had not forgotten his roots. And he never would.

Sammy Claus

Sammy is a hero in the Dominican Republic. His countrymen have followed his career almost from the day he signed his first professional contract. Children look up to Sammy. They see him as a shining example of what can be achieved through hard work and determination.

"Sammy is a wonderful kid," Manuel Rodriguez Robles, the former mayor of San Pedro de Macoris, told *The New York Times* in the summer of 1998. "What he has done is great for baseball, great for the Dominican Republic, and great for San Pedro de Macoris. He has projected this country and this town onto the world stage in a way that no Dominican has ever done."

Baseball has made Sammy rich and famous. But his popularity stems not just from his status as an athlete. He is a genuinely decent man who understands the importance of giving back to his community. Sammy lives in Chicago with his wife, Sonia, and their four young children during the baseball season. But he also has a

33

home in the Dominican Republic. Sammy and his family spend most of the winter there. He keeps a plaque in his living room bearing the following message: *"My house is small, no mansion for a millionaire. But there is room for love and there is room for friends."*

Sammy has never lost sight of the important things in life. He feels an obligation to help those less fortunate than himself. During the Christmas holiday season Sammy visits hospitals and delivers presents to children. He also purchases computers and other equipment for public schools. Kids in the Dominican Republic often refer to him as "Sammy Claus."

Sammy has invested heavily in his hometown. He has spent millions of dollars to build a shopping mall called 30–30 Plaza. The name reflects Sammy's status as the first Cub to hit 30 home runs and steal 30 bases in a single season. In the center of 30–30 Plaza is a wishing well. A statue of Sammy wearing his Cubs uniform rises above the well. A sign reads "Fountain of the Shoeshine Boys." All of the coins tossed into the fountain are donated to charitable causes.

And there's more. In 1997 Sammy opened a baseball school in his hometown. The school offers scholarships to underprivileged teenagers who have shown exceptional promise as baseball players. Students at the school receive free housing, food, training, and clothing. Sammy

personally works with many of the children. He offers advice on hitting, fielding, and following your dreams. Several graduates of the school have already been offered professional contracts.

Sammy is a generous man, and many people respect and admire him for that. But he tends to deflect the praise that comes his way. Sammy does not believe he should be congratulated for simply doing what is right. He sees poor children in the Dominican Republic, and he knows that many of them will have difficult lives. He also knows that things could have turned out much differently for him.

As it happened, Sammy was right in the middle of the home run derby when Hurricane Georges devastated parts of his homeland. He happened to be in Denver, playing the Colorado Rockies at the time. Right after his Saturday game, he went to the Dominican consulate to load trucks with goods for the hurricane relief effort.

"My life is kind of like a miracle," Sammy has often said. To him, giving back is a way of giving thanks.

Michael Who?

As spring gave way to summer, Sammy's popularity soared. A giant mural of Sammy was

hung above the Kennedy Expressway in Chicago. Sports fans all over the city stopped talking about basketball's Chicago Bulls — that city's winningest team. They stopped speculating about whether Michael Jordan would retire. Instead, they focused their attention on the Cubs, who were in the thick of a play-off race. And they saved their most lavish praise for Slammin' Sammy, the man whose smile could light up a ballpark in the dead of night.

Sammy has never hid his emotions. Fans love watching him sprint around the bases, pumping his fist and making all sorts of personal gestures. After each home run he thumps his chest with a fist and touches his fingers to his lips.

"This to show my appreciation to the fans here at Wrigley Field," Sammy explained. "The fans have been great to me. They support me so much. I don't know how to pay them back. I try to make them happy. They come to the ballpark because they know I am going to give one hundred percent and do everything to win the game. So, when I put my hand across my chest, it means I love you. When I hit a home run, I throw a kiss to my mother."

Sammy also sometimes raises his hand and forms the letter V for victory. That is in honor of the late Harry Caray, a longtime television and radio commentator whose voice was known and loved by millions of Cubs fans.

In 1998, it was hard to find anyone who didn't like Sammy Sosa. That included his biggest rival. Mark McGwire hit his 55th home run on August 30. The next day, Sammy hit number 55. By this time it was a two-man race. Griffey had fallen off the pace. Sammy continued to praise McGwire and to predict that Big Mac would probably win the Great Home Run Race. When Mark seemed to be wilting under the pressure of chasing Maris, Sammy even offered some advice. He urged Mark to loosen up and enjoy the ride.

And that's exactly what Mark did.

In the heat of the Great Home Run Race, he and Sammy proved that opponents could also be friends. "I know we're on different teams," Sammy said. "But we are still human beings, and I like and respect Mark."

6
62!

The Great Home Run Race of 1998 had a magical effect. It captured the imagination of people all over the country. Not just baseball fans. Not just sports fans.

Everyone.

Mark McGwire and Sammy Sosa are two of the game's finest players. They are also two of the game's finest men. It was almost impossible to root against either one of them. In fact, when the Cubs and Cardinals traveled, a strange thing occurred. Opposing fans cheered for them.

When the Cubs played a game against the Pirates at Pittsburgh's Three Rivers Stadium in

early September, Sammy received the warmest reception. Fans hung signs encouraging him to hit a home run. They even held up a banner designed to look like a giant bull's-eye!

If a pitcher failed to put the ball over the middle of the plate when either Sammy or Mark was batting, the stadium erupted in a chorus of boos. Everyone wanted to see a home run. They wanted to be part of history.

The media coverage surrounding Mark and Sammy reached a peak on Labor Day weekend, when more than six hundred reporters showed up for a series between the Cubs and the Cardinals. By then, Mark had already become only the third player in history to hit 60 home runs. Sammy had 58. Only 2 home runs separated the two sluggers. Now they would meet face-to-face. Their showdown was expected to be the highlight of an extraordinary season.

"It's going to be electrifying," Mark said before the series. "It's going to be exciting. If you can't be looking forward to these two games, then your heart is not beating."

Sammy was equally excited. "Mark and I are pushing each other," he said. "And we're not going to stop now."

Big Mac Attack

On Monday afternoon, September 7, the Cardinals hosted the Chicago Cubs at sold-out Busch Stadium. The children of Roger Maris were in the stands, as was Bud Selig, the commissioner of Major League Baseball.

They didn't have to wait long for something to happen. In the bottom of the first inning, Mark jumped on Mike Morgan's third pitch and drove the ball deep into the left-field stands. As Mark raised his arms in celebration, the crowd went wild! The record had been tied.

After rounding the bases, Mark hugged his son, Matt, a Cardinals batboy. In right field, Sammy Sosa smiled and clapped one hand into his mitt. Before disappearing into the dugout, Mark touched his chest with a fingertip and looked toward the sky. "I wanted the Maris family to know that Roger was with me," he later explained.

Mark also shouted "Happy birthday, Dad!" to his father, who was sitting in the stands. It was a wonderful present. On John McGwire's 61st birthday, Mark had hit his 61st home run.

Afterward, Sammy could only marvel at what a remarkable day it had been. He had fallen behind in the race, and it now looked as though Mark would surely be the one to break Maris'

record. But Sammy didn't seem to mind. "We just have to enjoy it and congratulate Mark," he said.

The bat that Maris used to hit his 61st homer had been flown from the Baseball Hall of Fame in Cooperstown, New York, to St. Louis. Before he took the field on Tuesday, September 8, Mark held the bat for good luck. "Roger," he whispered, "I hope you're with me tonight."

Everyone was with Mark, including Sammy Sosa. When Mark hit home run number 62 off Cubs pitcher Steve Trachsel in the fourth inning, Busch Stadium began to shake. An eleven-minute celebration followed. The new home run king was so excited that he almost forgot to touch first base. Mark shook hands with each of the Cubs infielders. He gave a big hug to third basemen Gary Gaetti, who had begun the season with the Cardinals.

Mark was greeted at home plate by his son. Then he was mobbed by his teammates. He even climbed into the stands to hug the Maris children. In a wonderful display of sportsmanship and friendship, Sammy Sosa jogged in from right field and embraced Mark. The two greatest sluggers in the game held each other for several moments. They were two men from strikingly different worlds. But history and baseball had brought them together. They would forever be linked.

"When he hugged me, it was a great moment," Sammy said. "I could see the emotion in Mark's eyes. This is a great moment for baseball, and everybody knows that. It's something I'm not going to forget."

Sammy's Turn

With Mark McGwire holding a 4-home-run lead over Sammy and less than three weeks remaining in the season, it appeared as though the race might be over. But Sammy wasn't quite through. He hit his 59th home run on September 11 and his 60th on September 12. Suddenly, he trailed Mark by only 2 home runs. The stage was now set for the biggest day of Sammy's career.

Wrigley Field was packed on Sunday, September 13, when the Cubs met the Milwaukee Brewers. The crowd of 40,846 was the largest of the season, and not simply because of Sammy. The Cubs were still battling the New York Mets for a wild card spot in the National League playoffs. For the first time in more than a decade, Cubs fans actually had something to cheer about in September.

They gave Sammy a standing ovation when he came to the plate in the fifth inning. And when he ripped an 0–1 pitch from Bronswell

Patrick 480 feet into the street beyond the left-field fence, the fans went wild. Sammy Sosa had hit his 61st home run of the year. He had tied Roger Maris!

And the day was far from over.

With one out in the ninth inning, Sammy came to the plate again. The Cubs trailed by a score of 10–8. Sammy was patient. He worked relief pitcher Eric Plunk until the count was two balls and one strike. The next pitch was a fastball, right down the middle. Sammy jumped on it. With the crowd chanting "Sixty-two! Sixty-two!" he drove the pitch deep into left field, just as he had in the fifth inning. The ball sailed high above the bleachers and out into the street.

Incredible! In one sun-soaked afternoon, Sammy had passed Babe Ruth and Roger Maris, and pulled even with Mark McGwire.

"It's unbelievable," Sammy said afterward. "It's something that even I can't believe I was doing. It can happen to two people, Mark and I."

The game was delayed for six minutes as the celebration raged on. Sammy came out of the dugout three times to tip his cap and wave to the crowd. Tears streamed down his face. "I don't usually cry, but today I was so emotional," Sammy said. "I have to say what I did is for the people of Chicago, for America, for my mother, for my wife, my kids, and the people I have

around me. My team. It was an emotional moment."

Best of all, Sammy's second homer cut Milwaukee's lead to just one run, 10–9. Gary Gaetti's RBI single later in the inning tied the score. And Mark Grace's solo homer in the 10th inning gave the Cubs an 11–10 victory and a one-game lead in the wild card race.

But the day belonged to Sammy, as Grace was quick to point out. "I thought the home run race was going to be McGwire's," Grace said. "But when my buddy gets hot, he can hit them in a hurry. And he proved that. I just hope Sammy gets the attention he deserves. Not only has he hit sixty-two homers, but he has carried us. He is without a doubt the MVP of the National League."

The numbers supported Grace's argument. Sammy now shared the single-season record for home runs. He had a league-leading 145 RBIs. And his batting average was an impressive .314. Sammy was having the best year of his career. In fact, he was putting together one of the best seasons that any player had ever had.

Thanks to Sammy's stunning outburst (4 home runs in three days), the home run race was wide open again. Sammy's only regret was that Mark McGwire had not been on the field to share the experience with him.

"Mark, you know I love you," Sammy said in a

postgame press conference. "I wish you could be here with me today. I know you are watching me, and I know you have the same feeling for me as I have for you in my heart."

Sammy paused and looked out over a sea of microphones and television cameras. He thumped his chest with his fist and said, "That's for you, Mark."

7

Down to the Wire

There was some controversy surrounding Sammy's record-breaking home runs. When Mark McGwire had surpassed Roger Maris, the entire country seemed to join in the celebration. The game was broadcast on national television. The commissioner of baseball was on hand to extend his congratulations. The Maris family had been flown in.

Major League Baseball even went to great lengths to make sure that the historic balls were properly marked and retrieved. All of the baseballs pitched to Mark in those final days were coated with a special invisible ink. When the balls were placed under infrared light, the ink

would glow. That way there would be no mistakes.

No such precautions were taken with Sammy Sosa. Sammy hit his 61st and 62nd home runs in a game that was broadcast only on local television. The commissioner of baseball was not at Wrigley Field, although he did place a phone call to Sammy after the game. The Maris family was absent, too.

"It's unfortunate," said Mark Grace. "Mark McGwire got so much more because he was the first to do it. Now it's like, 'Oh, by the way, Sammy has sixty-two homers, too.'"

Some newspaper columnists were quick to pass judgment on the situation. They rushed to Sammy's defense. They said that Mark McGwire had received more attention because of the color of his skin. Mark, of course, is white. Sammy is not.

When he heard about these accusations, Sammy moved quickly to put out the fire. His agent, Tom Reich, even wrote a letter to Major League Baseball officials. In the letter, Reich said that Sammy did not feel slighted. In fact, as Sammy had said after hitting number 62, he felt like the luckiest man in the world. "It is obvious that much of the media has chosen to make a significant issue out of possible attention to Mark McGwire at the expense of the spectacular young Sammy," Reich wrote. "We reject this notion." The

letter also thanked Major League Baseball "for the sensitivity, enthusiasm and many kindnesses that have been extended to Sammy."

The Cubs announced that Sammy would be honored at a special ceremony prior to the team's final home game of the season. And the commissioner of Major League Baseball promised to be there. For now, though, there were important matters to address. The Great Home Run Race, after all, was far from over.

Back and Forth

Mark McGwire and the Cardinals were in Houston on the day that Sammy hit number 62. When Mark heard about Sammy's feat, he smiled. "I think it's awesome," Mark said. "I've said a thousand times that I'm not competing against Sammy. I can only take care of myself. Imagine if we're tied at the end. What a beautiful way to end the season."

Mark then went out and took the field against the Astros. He grounded out twice before leaving the game with back spasms. Since hitting his 62nd home run, Mark had managed only one base hit in fourteen trips to the plate. He was mired in one of his worst slumps of the season. And now an old injury was flaring up. Maybe Sammy had the advantage.

"We'll see," Sammy said. "I'll tell you when the season is over."

By September 15, Mark was fit enough to regain the home run lead in the first game of a doubleheader against the Pittsburgh Pirates. It was a dramatic shot. Mark came off the bench as a pinch hitter in the ninth inning. He ripped Jason Christiansen's pitch over the wall in left-center field for his 63rd homer of the season.

But Sammy responded magnificently the very next night. His 63rd home run was an eighth-inning grand slam against the San Diego Padres. Sammy also had a two-run double in that game. He drove in all of his team's runs in a 6–3 victory that helped the Cubs maintain a slim lead over the Mets in the National League wild-card race. "I think sixty-two and sixty-three are pretty good for me," Sammy said. "Now I want to take my team to the play-offs."

Since the Cardinals weren't involved in a play-off race, Mark McGwire was able to concentrate only on hitting home runs. And, once again, he responded to Sammy, hitting number 64 on September 18 in Milwaukee's County Stadium. Mark belted a 3–1 pitch from rookie Rafael Roque 417 feet into the left-center-field bleachers for a two-run homer in the fourth inning.

Afterward, though, Mark once again tried to downplay the importance of finishing ahead of

Sammy. "We can't worry about each other," Mark said. "I mean, right now it's a big deal who finishes on top. But if you ask Sammy and I, I don't think it really matters."

Sammy's Big Day

September 20 was Sammy Sosa Day at Wrigley Field. It was one of the most emotional and uplifting events in the history of Chicago sports. That's saying a lot, when you consider that Chicago has thrown more than a few parties for its beloved Bulls and Michael Jordan.

Michael was here for this celebration, too — as a fan. "Sammy is the MVP, easily," Michael said. "I'm happy for him. And I think he's going to win the home run race."

The Cubs and Major League Baseball spared no expense. Sammy's mother, Lucrecya, was flown in from the Dominican Republic. So were his brothers and sisters. Hall of Fame pitcher Juan Marichal was there, too. That was important to Sammy, since Marichal is also a native of the Dominican Republic. He now serves as the country's secretary of sports.

All six of Roger Maris' children were present. So was Major League Baseball Commissioner Bud Selig, who presented Sammy with the Commissioner's Historic Achievement Award. "I

never want Sammy to think that he has been treated in any way but with the greatest respect," Selig said. "Here's a young man who battled from nothing and stayed with it. It's a wonderful story."

The party began with Cubs general manager Ed Lynch saying, "It's been one of the greatest individual seasons in the history of baseball. I don't think there's any way we could properly show our appreciation, but we're going to try."

The stands in Wrigley were dotted with banners and signs. One read, "Sammy: You're The Man!" Another, in Spanish, read, *"Sosa Para Presidente"* (Sosa for President). Fans were given Dominican flags on their way into the stadium, to help Sammy feel even more at home. The team pennants that usually wave in the breeze high above the stadium were replaced with Dominican flags. Latin music spiced up the entire affair. And the Dominican national anthem was played before the start of the game.

Sammy received several presents on this day, including a brand-new car. But perhaps the most meaningful gift came in the form of a simple letter:

Congratulations on your special day at Wrigley Field. We have shared an exciting and historic season that will be remembered for years

*to come. You have handled yourself with class
and dignity and are to be commended for a fan-
tastic 1998 season.*

Enjoy your day.

Sincerely, Mark McGwire

Sammy was deeply touched by the ceremony.
After receiving his gifts, he stepped up to a microphone and told the sellout crowd, "It's been
something special. Thank you very much and
God bless all of you." As his fans cheered enthu-
siastically, Sammy stepped away. He paused for
a moment before holding an index finger in the
air and returning to the microphone. "Excuse
me," Sammy said. "I forgot my family. My wife,
my mother, my brothers and friends. They've
supported me one hundred percent."

As the crowd roared again, Sammy hugged
his mother and kissed his wife. Then he hopped
into his new car and took a victory lap around
Wrigley Field as the theme song from the movie
Superman rumbled through the public address
system.

It almost didn't matter that the Cubs lost this
game. Or that Sammy did not hit a home run. It
didn't even matter that Mark McGwire hit number 65 that very afternoon. This day belonged to
Sammy Sosa.

Happy Endings

But the season, and the fireworks, were far from over. Although team spirit was foremost in Sammy's mind, still, he continued to smash homers. Lightning struck again on September 23, in a game against the Milwaukee Brewers. Slammin' Sammy earned his nickname by blasting numbers 64 and 65 out of the park.

Magical number 66 came on September 25 in the Houston Astrodome. At that exact moment in time, Mark McGwire had hit 65 homers — he'd deliver 66 the same day. But for a historic forty-five minutes, Sammy Sosa was ahead in the home run derby: the first and only time that would happen.

Best of all was that September 28, in a one game play-off with the San Francisco Giants to determine which team would be the wild card winner in the National League, Sammy led his team right into the play-offs. He is truly a home run hero and a team player.

Big Mac went on to win the Great Home Run Race with 70 homers. Sammy proudly took second place with 66. But Sammy's place in history is secure. He will always be known as one of the greatest sluggers in baseball.

Sammy will also be remembered for the way he carried himself with style and grace in the summer of 1998. And for the way he transformed an intense rivalry into a lifelong friendship.

#21 SAMMY SOSA

Chicago Cubs — Outfield • Bats: Right • Throws: Right
Height: 6'0" • Weight: 200 • Born: Nov. 12, 1968

YEAR	TEAM	AVG.	GAMES	AT BATS	RUNS	HITS	2B	3B	HR	RBI	BB	SO
1989	Rangers	.238	25	84	8	20	3	0	1	3	0	20
1989	White Sox	.273	33	99	19	27	5	0	3	10	11	27
1990	White Sox	.233	153	532	72	124	26	10	15	70	33	150
1991	White Sox	.203	116	316	39	64	10	1	10	33	14	98
1992	Cubs	.260	67	262	41	68	7	2	8	25	19	63
1993	Cubs	.261	159	598	92	156	25	5	33	93	38	135
1994	Cubs	.300	105	426	59	128	17	6	25	70	25	92
1995	Cubs	.268	144	564	89	151	17	3	36	119	58	134
1996	Cubs	.273	124	498	84	136	21	2	40	100	34	134
1997	Cubs	.251	162	642	90	161	31	4	36	119	45	174
1998	Cubs	.308	159	643	134	198	20	0	66	158	73	171
Total		.264	1247	4664	727	1233	182	33	273	800	350	1198

#	GM	DATE	PITCHER, CLUB	H/A	INN.	OB	DIST.
1	5	Apr. 4	M. Valdes, Mon.	H	3	0	371'
2	11	Apr. 11	A. Telford, Mon.	A	7	0	350'
3	14	Apr. 15	D. Cook, N.Y. (N)	A	8	0	430'
4	21	Apr. 23	D. Miceli, S.D.	H	9	0	420'
5	22	Apr. 24	I. Valdes, L.A.	A	1	0	430'
6	25	Apr. 27	J. Hamilton, S.D.	A	1	1	434'
7	30	May 3	C. Politte, Stl.	H	1	0	370'
8	42	May 16	S. Sullivan, Cin.	A	3	2	420'
9	47	May 22	G. Maddux, Atl.	A	1	0	440'
10	50	May 25	K. Millwood, Atl.	A	4	0	410'
11	50	May 25	M. Cather, Atl.	A	8	2	420'
12	51	May 27	D. Winston, Phi.	H	8	0	460'
13	51	May 27	W. Gomes, Phi.	H	9	1	400'
14	56	June 1	R. Dempster, Fla.	H	1	1	430'
15	56	June 1	O. Henriquez, Fla.	H	8	2	410'
16	58	June 3	L. Hernández, Fla.	H	5	1	370'
17	59	June 5	J. Parque, Chi. (A)	H	5	1	370'
18	60	June 6	C. Castillo, Chi. (A)	H	7	0	410'
19	61	June 7	J. Baldwin, Chi. (A)	H	5	2	380'
20	62	June 8	L. Hawkins, Min.	A	3	0	340'
21	66	June 13	M. Portugal, Phi.	A	6	1	350'
22	68	June 15	C. Eldred, Mil.	H	1	0	420'
23	68	June 15	C. Eldred, Mil.	H	3	0	410'
24	68	June 15	C. Edlred, Mil.	H	7	0	415'
25	70	June 17	B. Patrick, Mil.	H	4	0	430'
26	72	June 19	C. Loewer, Phi.	H	1	0	380'
27	72	June 19	C. Loewer, Phi.	H	5	1	380'
28	73	June 20	M. Beech, Phi.	H	3	1	366'
29	73	June 20	T. Borland, Phi.	H	6	2	500'
30	74	June 21	T. Green, Phi.	H	4	0	380'
31	77	June 24	S. Greisinger, Det.	A	1	0	390'

#	GM	DATE	PITCHER, CLUB	H/A	INN.	OB	DIST.
32	78	June 25	B. Moehler, Det.	A	7	0	400'
33	82	June 30	A. Embree, Ari.	H	8	0	364'
34	88	July 9	J. Juden, Mil.	A	2	1	432'
35	89	July 10	S. Karl, Mil.	A	2	0	428'
36	95	July 17	K. Ojala, Fla.	A	6	1	440'
37	100	July 22	M.Batista, Mon.	H	8	2	365'
38	105	July 26	R. Reed, N.Y. (N)	H	6	1	420'
39	106	July 27	W. Blair, Ari.	A	6	1	350'
40	106	July 27	A.Embree, Ari.	A	8	3	420'
41	107	July 28	B. Wolcott, Ari.	A	5	3	400'
42	110	July 31	J. Wright, Col.	A	1	0	371'
43	114	Aug. 5	A. Benes, Ari.	H	3	1	374'
44	117	Aug. 8	R. Croushore, Stl.	A	9	1	400'
45	119	Aug. 10	R. Ortiz, S.F.	A	5	0	370'
46	119	Aug. 10	C. Brock, S.F.	A	7	0	480'
47	124	Aug. 16	S. Bergman, Hou.	A	4	0	360'
48	126	Aug. 19	K. Bottenfield, St.L.	H	5	1	368'
49	128	Aug. 21	O. Hershiser, S.F.	H	5	1	415'
50	130	Aug. 23	J. Lima, Hou.	H	5	0	440'
51	130	Aug. 23	J. Lima, Hou.	H	8	0	388'
52	133	Aug. 26	B. Tomko, Cin.	H	8	0	438'
53	135	Aug. 28	J. Thomson, Col.	A	1	0	414'
54	137	Aug. 30	D. Kile, Col.	A	1	1	482'
55	138	Aug. 31	B. Tomko, Cin.	H	3	1	364'
56	138	Sept. 2	J. Bere, Cin.	H	0	1	370'
57	139	Sept. 4	J. Schmidt, Pitt.	A	0	1	400'
58	142	Sept. 5	S. Lawrence, Pitt.	A	6	0	405'
59	148	Sept. 11	B. Pulsipher, Mil.	H	5	0	435'
60	149	Sept. 12	V. De Los Santos, Mil.	H	7	2	430'
61	150	Sept. 13	B. Patrick, Mil.	H	5	1	480'
62	150	Sept. 13	E. Plunk, Mil.	H	9	0	480'

#	GM	DATE	PITCHER, CLUB	H/A	INN.	OB	DIST.
63	153	Sept. 16	B. Boehringer, S.D.	A	8	3	434'
64	158	Sept. 23	R. Roque, Mil.	A	5	0	344'
65	158	Sept. 23	R. Henderson, Mil.	A	6	0	410'
66	160	Sept. 25	J. Lima, Hou.	A	4	0	420'

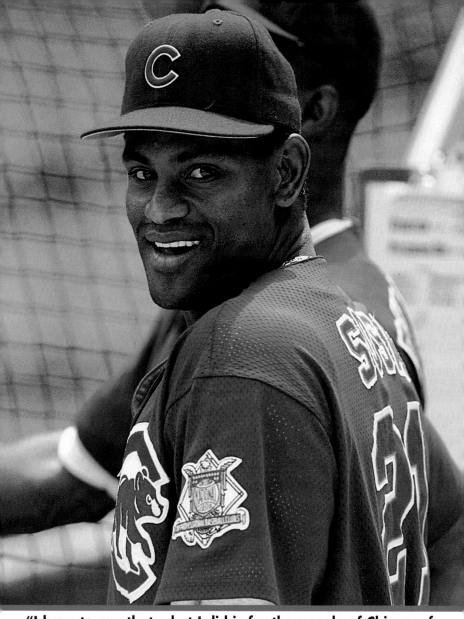

"I have to say that what I did is for the people of Chicago, for America, for my mother, for my wife, my kids, and the people I have around me. My team. It was an emotional moment."
—Sammy Sosa

...and slides into home.

Number 21,
Sammy struts
his stuff in the
outfield...

September 13, 1998.
Sosa is carried off the field
following his record tying
62nd homer against the
Milwaukee Brewers in
Chicago's Wrigley Field.

Sosa slams another homer in his quest for the record.

Slammin' Sammy jumps up in the air after launching a tiebreaking grand slam to pull even with McGwire at 63 home runs.

The fans know Sammy is without a doubt the National League's Most Valuable Player.